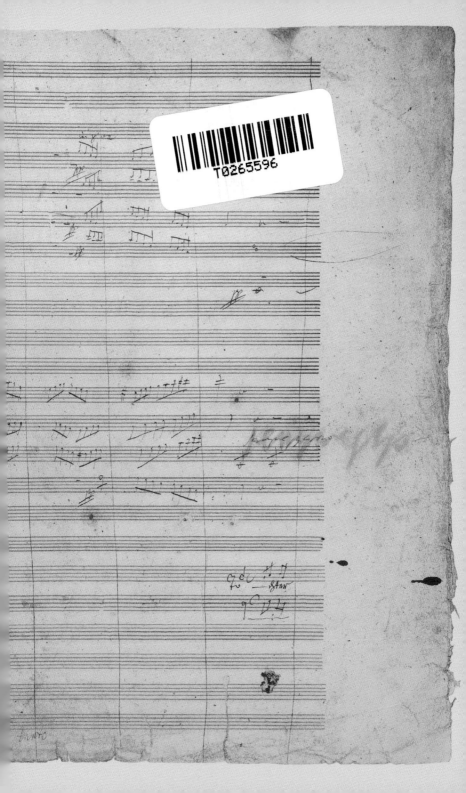

Franz Welser-Möst

From Silence
Finding Calm in a Dissonant World

Franz Welser-Möst

With Axel Brüggemann
Translated by Christine Shuttleworth

Dedicated to my dear wife, Geli

From Silence

Finding Calm
in a Dissonant World

I. The teaching of music
On the implicitness of sound

II. The places of music
On the organisation of sound

III. Markets of music
On the consumption of sound

IV. Artists and music
On the production of sound

Preface and acknowledgments

Extraordinary!

When, in August 2019, Brandstätter Verlag approached me to ask if I wanted to write a book, I was not sure if I should do so. Then we found the right partner in Axel Brüggemann, who was ready to record my thoughts. During the following December we met regularly, and as a result of these meetings a working title for the book rapidly crystallised: Out of the Silence. And then came the coronavirus, and the whole world stood still. Extraordinary – a coincidence?

I write these words during the first days of the complete shutdown in Austria. A kind of involuntary and forced retreat from the world. A dreadful way to be forced to rest. At present, no one can foresee how the situation will develop. But my great hope is that at the end of this global crisis, which will undoubtedly claim many victims, we will be able to breathe a sigh of relief again. And that after this sigh of relief, there will remain a consciousness of silence, and that our self-denial will be understood as an opportunity to question the essential and even perhaps to create a new order – individually and as a society.

At first I was not sure about the aims of this book, but while working on it I became increasingly aware that it is also intended as a guide for the next generations of musicians – to give them courage not to be dazzled by early successes and by no means to allow themselves to be corrupted. To them and to all readers, I would like to offer the thought that even an outwardly successful life consists of many highs and lows, of curves where one does not know what awaits one around the bend. Streamlined careers have always been suspect to me.

My accident of 1978 is an involuntary symbol of this: the car came off the road, and after this dramatic event a huge effort was needed to find my way back into life. I want to encourage others to believe in their own talents, to stand up for their convictions, which they have developed by means of searching and digging, even if this does not correspond to the spirit of the times – as well as not to jump onto any bandwagon which stands ready for us in our present-day culture of permanent excitement. Many experiences which are painful in the moment later turn out to represent important and appropriate changes of course. I am thankful for the great moments and wonderful encounters that accompany the life of an artist.

This book is also an appeal to us creative artists not to take our profession for granted, as a benefit to our vanity and our pockets, but to invest creatively in the future.

The book is a partly humorous, but also deeply serious journey through my 60 years, in which I have learned to question many things, and to appreciate everything, really everything, that happens to me. And to learn, learn, learn.

My gratitude is due to Brandstätter Verlag, who came up with the idea and have accompanied me attentively through the period during which this book came into being.

But above all to Axel Brüggemann, who, in several intensive conversations, was able to unearth much out of my innermost being which I had not intended to share with the public, an eloquent and brilliant motivator who succeeded in bringing me to the point of doing so.

Special thanks also go to Annette Frank, who accompanied me intensively, expertly, patiently, but also stubbornly through the long process of corrections.

For the English version of the book my special thanks go to Clearview Books, to the Cleveland Orchestra, in particular to André Gremillet and Mark Williams and to my friend and agent Kathryn Enticott for their great support.

Prelude

This existential silence

To this day I am unable to say for sure whether I was aware that our car tyres had lost their grip on the frozen asphalt on the bridge to the Austrian village of Losenstein. We slid helplessly over an embankment and a few seconds later, after turning over a couple of times, came to a halt. Neither do I now remember whether I was able, from the back seat, to observe the driver trying to correct the sliding motion by energetically applying the brakes, which only made our situation worse. What, however, I do remember is that I perceived these seconds as an eternity.

Time seemed to dissolve, as did gravity. At that moment, the coordinate system that normally supports a human existence lost its meaning. In films, the subjective feeling during such an accident is often represented by the director showing the event in slow motion, with the vehicle's lurching action repeated over and over again from different perspectives.

The film that was playing in my head at that time was more like a radio play. Or rather, a dumb-show. I do not remember whether any words were uttered in our car, whether anyone whispered 'Oh God!' or shouted 'Look out!' I was conscious of the sliding of the car before the crash, but everything else around me suddenly seemed unreal. What I do remember is the unbelievable silence that surrounded me.

A silence that had nothing to do with the peace that I know from my many wanderings, when I am on my way in the mountains at sunrise, listening to the full orchestration of nature: leaves swaying in the wind, animals awakening in the darkness, the storm blowing in the treetops, or – within me – the rhythm of my own heartbeat. The silence of which I was aware on the back seat of our car sounded different. A silence that I had previously experienced, if at all, in music: a suspension of time and space. But in contrast to music, I was not able to shape this silence, to determine its structure or its duration – I was completely at its mercy, unable to move, let alone to influence what would happen in the seconds ahead. This silence seemed to me to ignore all the known rules of our world. A silence of seconds or an eternal silence – I cannot say, since even time itself was annihilated, extending, as it were, into infinity. The silence I heard in our car while it slid out of control over the asphalt was a silence that was more silent than anything that I had not heard up to then.

Since that day I have thought repeatedly about the phenomenon of silence. Silence as the opportunity to bring to mind the omnipresent intensity of sound of the world. Silence as a condition of absence of sound. Is it not the definition of silence that there are sounds at its beginning and end? Is silence not actually the area of tension between two poles of sound, the condition between the audible, which ultimately defines a silence that prevails at any time?

In the Bible, angels proclaim the message of God. To proclaim to the world implies that one is oneself surrounded by silence. For humans too, hearing and not hearing are existential conditions of perception of the world. It is not for nothing that we speak of standing *still*. It is the sense of hearing that we perhaps trust the least. That sense that, conditioned by evolution, never sleeps: while we close our eyes, our ears remain alert, warning us about tigers or wolves, even when the rest of the body has long been 'turning a deaf ear'.

The silence that I experienced in our car just before the accident had nothing negative about it. I could not however say that I found it 'beautiful'; perhaps 'satisfying' would be a more appropriate adjective. A satisfying vacuum of sound. This was what surrounded me when the first impact of the overturning vehicle robbed me of consciousness and we came to a standstill on a frozen field in the foothills of the Austrian Alps.

Later, in the hospital, when I had been moved to the general ward after a few days in the intensive care unit, I was handed one of the light blue pillows which were popular at that time in Austrian hospitals, with a loudspeaker sewn into them. The first music I heard was Schubert's Mass in G major, which was being transmitted from the Österreich 1 (Ö1) radio station. Schubert had composed it at only 18 years of age.

***

On 19 November 1978, the day of the accident, I was also 18 years old. And I was well on the way to realising my greatest dream: I wanted to become a professional violinist – preferably with the Vienna Philharmonic. Together with friends, I had just performed Schubert's Mass in G major at the ceremonial Mass in Großraming, in Upper Austria. The performance took place in the church, whose oldest parts date from the year 1513 and which is dedicated to St James. Großraming was the birthplace of my teacher, Balduin Sulzer, and it was his brother, Otto Sulzer, the leader of the local church choir, who had asked us to play the Mass.

One hundred and fifty years earlier, on 19 November 1828, Franz Schubert was battling typhoid fever in his brother Ferdinand's apartment in Vienna. He lost the battle and died around 3pm, aged only 31. The day of his death was to define our Sunday. From Großraming we had planned to drive on to Steyr. This was where Schubert had begun to compose his Trout Quintet, which we also planned to perform later. After our successful performance of the High Mass at the church, we had first of all fortified ourselves at the Kirchenwirt restaurant in the village. Our group consisted of the local church choir and the orchestra, which also included some students at the Linz *Musikgymnasium* (a secondary school specialising in music). It also included the family of a businessman, who were friends of mine – the father was an enthusiastic amateur cellist. It was with him, his wife, his son and two girls who were schoolmates of the son that I planned later to travel the 40 kilometres or so to Steyr, along the river Enns through the beautiful Enns valley.

When we left the Kirchenwirt, I heard the father, as he passed his son the car keys, warning him: 'Be careful, the bridges could be icy.' The son, who had passed his driving test only half a year earlier, nodded. Then we got into the Mercedes, to drive through the foothills of the Austrian Alps. I sat in the back, on the right. His mother was seated next to me, with her husband on her left. The two schoolgirls were next to the son, who was at the wheel. We had been on the road for a good ten minutes when – it was three pm exactly – we drove across the bridge at Losenstein and the car began to lurch about. The driver, as I have mentioned, tried to avoid the worst by hitting the brakes, which however caused the car to lose control entirely. Everything that happened after that, I know only from the accounts of others.

That evening, my parents wanted to attend the concert, and in the late afternoon they called in on the family of our friends. There, a relative of the family gave them the sad news: 'But didn't you know? There has been an accident. The lady died on the spot, and all the others are in the hospital.' This was a shock for my parents, and they immediately made their way to the hospital.

Later I was told that some of the members of the choir, who had been driving directly behind our car, had witnessed the accident. One of them was also a fireman, and he pulled us out of the wreck. When, still at the scene, I recovered consciousness, my first thought was: 'I hope we will get to the concert on time.' Today I find it comforting how gracious nature is in trying to repress the almost unbearable. Together with the son of the family, I was taken to hospital in an ambulance.

When, after receiving first aid, I was taken to the intensive care unit, I experienced excruciating pain in my back. 'What's wrong with me?' I asked the nurse who was looking after me, and who replied 'sensitively', 'You've broken three vertebrae.'

When I tried to move my feet, it was difficult at first, and I started to wonder what my life would be like in a wheelchair. My body recovered fairly quickly, but the accident was to affect my life in many respects for a long time. It turned out that the movement of two of my fingers had become irreversibly restricted, since the nerves were damaged. As a result, I had to give up my great dream of a career as a violinist. Then there was the pain, which accompanied me almost daily for nearly 14 years. Often it was so bad that I could hardly get out of bed in the morning, because my back was so cramped with tension. And it was also the experience of this accident that left its mark on me, this silence extending into infinity. At 18 years old I had encountered death, and this changed my life as has no experience before or since.

Since then I have given much thought to the strange aspects of this 19th of November. That our car came off the road exactly 150 years after Schubert's death, at exactly three pm, the time when the composer died. That the accident happened, of all times, after we had played Schubert's Mass in G major, which he had written at the age of 18, the same age that I was then. That we had planned to play his Trout Quintet, and that Schubert's music was the first I heard from the hospital pillow – again the Mass in G major! Was all this accidental, coincidental? In principle, I do not believe in coincidence. However, this 19th of November was certainly a day of accident, when so much happened to me which permanently changed my life. That Sunday was a fateful day for me, to which I owe much of what I am today.

✳✳✳

I still ask myself if the mother of my friends' family who died also heard that silence that I experienced before the accident – and if that silence was a forerunner of what awaits us after death. The rest of us, the survivors, were further affected by the terrible crash: the businessman's firm collapsed, and the son whose mother died by my side became seriously ill. Was everything that happened to us that Sunday in November simply an 'accident'?

In my case, the principal result of the accident was to change my attitude to death and to faith – that faith which my parents practised and which so deeply characterised our family. Later I searched for something else in different religions, in Buddhism and Hinduism, in Gandhi and Lao-Tzu. In the course of my wanderings through various religions I attained realisations which I found predominantly in philosophical writings. If anything, I would describe myself as an agnostic who follows Socrates, that is, someone who believes in the immortality of what we call the soul. This knowledge makes a very personal spirituality possible for me. It is nature above all which today gives me leisure and calm, and what is meant by spirituality is what I perhaps experience most in music.

Is it not significant that Franz Schubert composed his Mass in G major in only a week, and in the Credo, at only 18 years old, omitted the phrase *Et unam sanctam catholicam et apostolicam ecclesiam*, thus denying the statement of faith in the 'holy, catholic and apostolic Church'? Is it not also fascinating that he also left out the sentence, *Et exspecto resurrectionem mortuorum*, 'I await the resurrection of the dead'? The Mass in G major was the last music I heard before the accident – and it was the same music with which the world welcomed me back. Coincidence?

What I believe in is perhaps precisely that silence that I have experienced since then, the silence surrounded by sound. It is my form of eternity and otherworldliness. In it I find the consolation that at the end of a life, a feeling of contentment can set in. Perhaps this state can also be called silence of the soul. A state that I continually hope for in music. That I perhaps even pursue. A state that unfortunately occurs only very seldom, but when it does, it becomes a sort of epiphany.

I have experienced the existential greatness of music, for example, when I heard the pianist Radu Lupu's interpretation of Beethoven's Waldstein Sonata in the Zurich Tonhalle. I cannot describe exactly what this evening released in me, but I can say that I was unable to sleep for three nights afterwards, so shaken was I by what I had heard.

After the concert I visited Radu Lupu in his dressing room and said to him: 'I will probably remember this interpretation for the rest of my life.' I had the feeling that he himself was surprised by the effect of his playing. But his dry response was: 'Yes, that is probably what Beethoven intended.'

There are some performances which lead us beyond the limits of our existence and in which all participants become as one. The first time this happened to me was during the performance of Franz Schmidt's *Book with Seven Seals* at the abbey church at Wilhering, which I conducted at the age of 22. The Revelation of St John, which deals with precisely the 'Four Last Things' of human life, became a resounding image of the world. When I met my parents after the performance, neither they nor I could utter a word, and tears were running down my face.

It is above all the music of Schubert which has repeatedly led me, both as a listener and a performer, into these realms of crossed borders. A special memory for me is of a performance of the Schubert Quintet, which I played with friends during my time as principal conductor at Norrköping in Sweden (I had taken over the viola part despite my two damaged fingers). In the recapitulation of the second movement I suddenly heard and felt this music of eternity. Sounds in which all time is dissolved, music in which five musicians lose themselves in the moment of playing. Schubert composed this otherworldly music two months before his death, and perhaps this second movement comes closest to that silence which I heard before our car overturned.

Also unforgettable to me is a Schubert lieder evening, sung by Simon Keenlyside at the Schubertiade, in Schwarzenberg in Austria in 2002. Here too I was so overcome by the existential greatness of the music that afterwards I acquired the recording made by the ORF, the Austrian broadcaster, and have repeatedly listened to it.

On the occasion of my 50th birthday, as a sort of present to myself, I invited about 120 friends and acquaintances to a private 'Schubertiade'. Radu Lupu played Schubert's last piano sonata in

B flat major. Next, Simon Keenlyside sang some Schubert lieder, accompanied at the piano by Malcolm Martineau. Just before his appearance, Keenlyside asked me how, after such intensive music-making, it was at all possible to add and sing any other music.

And then there was the performance of Schubert's Great C Major Symphony, together with the Cleveland Orchestra in Cleveland on Friday 13 March 2020. It was at this point in time that the Covid-19 crisis was just beginning to grip the whole world. We all sensed that we were in an unprecedented, exceptional situation. We thus took the decision not to undertake any further public appearances of our orchestra. However, in order to be able to complete our current recording project (NB: the CD/download and streaming series *A New Century* with live recordings from Severance Hall), we performed the symphony in front of some 20 staff members from our office. Like a sword of Damocles, the question hovered over us as to whether and when we would again be able to make music together. This gave the performance a depth and at the same time a sense of weightlessness that I had never before experienced with this orchestra.

There are moments one yearns for as a musician, those little moments of eternity, in which the silence is filled with perfect music. Moments that are so precious because they occur so incredibly rarely.

If my life has a leitmotif, it is probably the fulfilment of silence, which, today in particular, forms an antithesis to the fast pace of our existence. Pausing in silence as a form of contemplation, as an alternative to the restless speed of our time. Silence as compensation for the decibelisation of our world.

Incidentally, after somewhat protracted legal proceedings, I was awarded damages of 120,000 Austrian schillings for the injuries I had suffered from the traffic accident. I had never had so much money at my disposal before – and I did not have it for long. I invested a large portion of it in long-playing records, including several different recordings of the *Missa solemnis* – and in a variety of scores. And in much music, after the silence.

I. The teaching of music

On the implicitness of sound

Born in music

Music was still something taken for granted in the world into which I was born. Between the world wars Austria had lost its old role in the European power structure. After the First World War, the First Republic had to relinquish large areas of Austria–Hungary, and many citizens of the former imperial and royal monarchy realised that history always involves change. When the fatherland totters, it is often faith that promises mankind an apparently stable system of coordinates. My parents met at the time when these in-between years in Austria came to a sinister end with the *Anschluss* to Hitler's Germany.

The plot of land on the Attersee where, replacing the dilapidated summerhouse, I built the house where my wife and I live today, once belonged to my father's father. Only a kilometre away, the family of my mother, who actually came from Wels, had a holiday home. Usually, the families met at the summer Masses at the chapel in nearby Buchberg, an idyllic little church for a congregation of about 100. It had been built in the 16th century by the Mondsee monastery. When my parents first met, which must have been in 1939, my mother was all of 14 years old and my father was 17. My grandmother played the go-between, unhesitatingly inviting my mother, Maria Elisabeth Wetzelsberger, known to all as Marilies, to the fruit harvest, where she and Franz Möst were eventually to get to know each other better.

The bell of the Buchberg church, which I can hear from my terrace, is incidentally still rung every day by hand – a sign not only of piety, but of the traditional nature of the region.

The author's parents, Marilies and Franz Möst: mid-1950s, Attersee

Although my father was not born until after the First World War, he grew up with the ideals of the old Austria: for God, Emperor and the Fatherland. At the same time, his faith was his most important compass. This was why he was a vigorous opponent of Hitler, the *Anschluss* of Austria, and the politics of the Nazi party.

My father worked with like-minded people in the Catholic resistance, but was soon discovered. A friend of the family, who had joined the Nazi party early on, came to my grandparents one day and reported that the party was conducting statistics on traitors to the people, and that my father had already collected two 'black marks'. On the third occasion, whether he liked it or not, he would end up in a camp. As the only way out of the situation, the friend suggested that my father should volunteer to join the Army. Which was what he did.

Today it is hardly imaginable how noisy the war years must have been. For my father, a time of catastrophes was beginning. In 1940, his father died; in 1941 he was stationed with the Wehrmacht, first in Stettin, then in Vaasa in Finland, then for eighteen months in Lofoten, at the time the most northern outpost of the German Army. After an odyssey from Landsberg am Lech, via Neiße on the river Neiße and Groß Born in Pomerania, to Prague, he was then, in January 1944, summoned to the battle of Monte Cassino. Here, 80,000 German soldiers fought 105,000 Allied troops around the monastery, which lies on a 516-metre-high rocky hill. The battle is known from the somewhat idealised film version, starring Joachim Fuchsberger, *Die grünen Teufel von Monte Cassino*, and by the fact that German troops brought the 1,200 historic books and the priceless paintings by Leonardo da Vinci, Titian and Raphael from the Benedictine monastery to Rome, to Castel Sant'Angelo in the Vatican. What is often hushed up is the discovery of 13 masterpieces found after the war in the tunnel of the salt mine at Altaussee, where Hitler had stored his art collection. Above all, however, the battle of Monte Cassino – like so many in the Second World War – was brutal and bloody. The four-month-long battle cost the lives of 20,000 German and 55,000

Allied soldiers. My father was taken prisoner and brought via Bari to a prisoner-of-war camp in Egypt.

My father was a prolific correspondent; he wrote poems and kept a diary. From his records I know that after the war ended on 23 August 1945 he was at last allowed to return to Linz. He had been through a great deal, and his health was severely affected. At first he was sent to a sanatorium for lung patients to recuperate. He began studying law, but eventually decided on studying medicine. Of all the things to happen, just when normality had returned to the point when my parents could have married, my mother's father died, and my parents, following the strict Catholic ordinance, had to observe a year of mourning. In 1954, the moment finally arrived. Marilies Wetzelsberger, who had in the meantime been studying soil culture in Vienna, and the graduate physician Franz Möst were able to enter the married state for which they had been waiting so long. And it is fair to say that my parents soon made up for lost time. My eldest brother Johannes was born in September 1956, my brother Thomas in November 1957, and my elder sister Maria a year later.

There is a family story about my birth: when, on 16 August 1960, my grandmother was asked by her neighbour over the fence whether a boy or a girl had been born, she burst into tears and sobbed: 'Both!' And indeed no one had realised that my mother was pregnant with twins, and it was a huge surprise to everyone when, immediately after my birth, my sister Elisabeth came into the world.

At first we lived in a two-room apartment in Linz, but when I was three years old we moved to my grandmother's house in Wels. By this time my father was working as a pulmonary specialist, and commuted daily to Schloss Cumberland in Gmunden, the same sanatorium for lung patients where he had been a patient after the war. It had been built in the finest Tudor style above the Krottensee by Ernst August, Crown Prince of Hanover. My father sometimes worked more than 120 hours a week, without actually earning a fortune. My mother dreamed of a second degree in law after her first qualification in soil culture, but for the time being – also because her father was ill for so long – she stayed at home.

I remember our living conditions at the time. We did not consider ourselves poor, but could not afford much. Up to 1970 we did not even have a television. Our entertainment consisted to a great extent in making our own music. My mother was a first-class pianist, and I still remember that we children often used to beg her in the evenings: '*Mutti*, please play some more for us.' My father had played the violin and trumpet as a child, and all my siblings had also learnt to play instruments. Music has always been an essential part of life for me. It was inconceivable to me as a child that there were people for whom making music was not part of the course of their day. For my parents, music was a sort of home refuge, a constant at a time which was marked by so many changes. Music was uplifting for them; it gave them a canon of values, and was in harmony with their religious faith.

The brilliantly white parish church in the centre of Wels (it is dedicated to the saint whose name is borne by my eldest brother, Johannes) has become for me a place where my longing for music is fulfilled. Apart from my mother's piano playing at home, I seldom had access to public musical performances. On the wooden benches in the church – always dressed by my mother in a Sunday suit or the white robe of the altar boy – I heard for the first time the Masses of Joseph Haydn, Franz Schubert and Wolfgang Amadeus Mozart. And I remember the ceremonial Masses that I experienced as a server from the ages of six to 14, and which could transport me into hitherto unknown spheres. During the Masses time seems to stand still and the noise of the world arranged itself into harmonies. What particularly impressed me as a child was that the priest insisted on allowing himself to be replaced at the altar by a retired minister, so that he could conduct the music of the Mass on major feast days.

Ultimately, it is to my parents' faith and their attachment to the church that I owe my first music lesson.

Franz Welser-Möst and his twin sister Elisabeth swimming in the Attersee in 1964

Sister Gerburga's ruler

My love of the violin was not a case of love at first sight. For standing between it and myself was Sister Gerburga. It was one of my father's principles that his children should not be taught at a public music school but – as in our case – at a Catholic convent school. So, from the age of six, I regularly attended the villa next to the convent school in Wels, where Sister Gerburga received her pupils: a gaunt, careworn woman. Sister Gerburga had already taught several classes of students over the years in Wels, not only the violin, but also instruments including the recorder, the guitar, accordion and cello. There was probably nothing that Sister Gerburga could not teach. In her strict manner, largely devoid of empathy, she embodied the stereotype of the frustrated woman who probably had not willingly chosen this life for herself or the anachronistically provincial ideal of education of the postwar era.

When I went to my lesson with my three-quarter-length violin under my arm, I knew that Sister Gerburga would always have her wooden ruler within easy reach. Whenever she felt like it, she would punish her students by rapping their fingers or hands with it. Reasons were easily found: wrong notes, awkward bowing, or simply just a self-conscious answer. Whether a lesson was going to go relatively well could usually be understood by Sister Gerburga's expression when she greeted us. She made no pretence about her mood, and one did not have the impression that she enjoyed her work or the progress of her students. One of her educational methods was to keep a so-called performance register. In this she kept a record of poor performances, which had to be countersigned at home by the student's mother. Very poor performances, however, had to be countersigned by the father. This says a great deal about the nun's world view, but perhaps also about Catholic Upper Austria of the late 1960s.

I did not, however, only go to violin lessons, but was also active as an altar boy. During Advent I had to get up very early for this duty. The Rorate Mass was held as early as 5.45am, after which I went home briefly to drink cocoa. Once a week at 6.30am I had my violin lesson with Sister Gerburga, and school began at 8am.

I clearly remember a hot day in June 1968, when I entered Sister Gerburga's classroom and realised that the blinds had been drawn. I could sense the cold sweat of the previous pupils in the air, and that day I tried particularly hard to play my exercises properly. But I began to feel more and more unwell. For fear of showing weakness, or of provoking Sister Gerburga's anger, I tried to suppress my urge to vomit, which in the end I failed to do. And so, in a great torrent, I threw up into my violin. Sister Gerburga held her compassion in check. She abruptly tore the violin from my hand and held the wood under running water to rinse away my vomit. Then she sent me home. It was the robustness of her manner that made me dream of never again having to attend a violin lesson.

After four years my father finally understood how I felt and allowed me to change to the city music school. I was ten years old when I acquired a new violin teacher, August Patzelt. He came from a completely different universe from Sister Gerburga. Among others, he played with the music tutor, conductor, biographer of Mozart and co-founder of the Salzburg Festival, Bernhard Paumgartner, in the Camerata Salzburg. His musical biography alone made it clear that my teacher had a broader outlook , that making music was not just a random profession for him, but a true vocation. August Patzelt was curious about us, his students, and encouraged us as much as he was able. After a year of studying with him, I was also allowed to play in the city's music school orchestra. Here another entirely new world opened up to me. The sound that we created together by means of pieces by Leopold Mozart and later, among others, of Edvard Grieg's *Holberg Suite*, overwhelmed me. And so I began to love playing the violin.

Away from my music studies, however, I remained a rather dreamy child, so much so that my mother worried about me. 'What is wrong with the boy? Why is he so quiet?' While my twin sister smoothly navigated her school career, I was not especially interested in all that. I was not a bad pupil, but did not learn very much. As a rule I looked forward to Thursdays, when I was allowed to go to the church library. I would take five or six books home with me, which I would then read over the following week. My favourites were sagas about heroes, or classic books for children and young people. The only books that did not appeal to me were Karl May's adventure novels.

These books became my actual world. I lived entirely within the universe of my imagination, and I often failed to notice that the real world was passing me by. It was at this time that my mother read an article in the local newspaper, the *Oberösterreichische Nachrichten*, which reported that a new Musikgymnasium, a secondary school specialising in music, was to be opened in Linz. Perhaps this would be a good opportunity for her dreamy son? And indeed, my years in

Linz at the Musikgymnasium with my future teacher, Balduin Sulzer, were to become unbelievably formative years in my musical life – and a practical lesson in what musical education should be about.

But before I report on this, here is a positive story about the convent school. The house where I had my violin lessons now belongs to some good friends of mine. And I had to chuckle when I visited them about ten years ago. The room where Sister Gerburga tormented me and her other students with her notion of music teaching is now my friends' bedroom – one can't imagine what Sister Gerburga would have thought of that.

Every child in Cleveland: the 100-year plan

Today I know that what I experienced as a child was not to be taken for granted – neither in the 1960s and 1970s, and certainly not today. For my parents, music meant home and stability, and they spurred me on to ask questions, to be curious and to approach the world with open ears. Today it is clear to me that I must accept that music, which means almost everything to me – particularly classical music – means little or even nothing to many people. What I took for granted for a lifetime plays no part in their lives.

I am not a fanatical missionary for music. But I firmly believe that music should be a human right, and that it provides enormous support in times of instability. That music is a place where we listen to each other and have a sense of each other. That music is a wonderful 'social cement' [Adorno]. As a child I grew up with the experience that when the world seems a little muddled, disorganised and chaotic, when the noise becomes too loud, in such moments the world can get great benefit from music. Because sound gives us a consciousness of silence, in which order can be possible. I do not want to convert anyone to music, but I want everyone to have the opportunity to experience music.

When I was asked in 1999 if I would like to become music director of the Cleveland Orchestra, I asked for time to think about it, which many people did not understand. As a basic principle I have no interest in quick, short-term commitments, and like to examine offers to decide whether there are good reasons for a long-term cooperation. I try to imagine whether I would still have something to say to an orchestra in five, ten or 20 years' time. Whether there is the potential for a continuing mutual development – both in terms of work on the sound and the repertoire, and of the social role of the orchestra in its local setting.

I thought seriously about it, and it quickly became clear to me that Cleveland was a city which had gone through the painful experience that history always cites as change, in which change is not an upward trajectory. It was once the fifth largest city in the USA, the flagship of industrialisation at the start of the 20th century. Its position on the northern edge of Ohio, on the shores of Lake Erie, was geographically favourable for the steel industry. And the Cleveland Orchestra, founded in 1918, had always been there for the citizens. An institution of which one was proud. In the 1960s it was still common practice for Cleveland people to welcome the musicians at the airport when they came back from a foreign tour.

However, for almost 100 years now Cleveland has been in recession. Unemployment increased at a frantic pace, especially when the steel industry suffered severe setbacks. At some point Cleveland acquired the nickname 'The Mistake on the Lake'. At the present time, 51 cities in the USA are larger than Cleveland. It now has a population of only 385,000, and the outflow from the city continues. In addition, there is hardly a city in the USA which has been devastated in the same way by racial conflict. Today, in 2020, some 53.3 per cent of the population is African American, 37.3 per cent white and 20 per cent Latino. Before the onset of the coronavirus crisis, unemployment stood at 7.3 per cent.

When I came to Cleveland for the first time as a guest conductor, I was startled by the desolate condition of the city. So it was even more astonishing to me that for over 100 years now its citizens have been able to afford one of the best orchestras in the world. Over the years I have discovered more and more of the beauties of this city and learned to appreciate the people who live in it.

So when the Cleveland Orchestra rings up, one does not say simply 'no'. But it was important to me to know why I should say 'yes'. The Cleveland Orchestra impressed me with its exceptional quality, formed by, among others, my predecessors Erich Leinsdorf (1943-1946), George Szell (1946-1970), Lorin Maazel (1972-1982), and Christoph von Dohnányi (1984-2002), and its great tradition. Another significant aspect apart from the qualitative development of the orchestral sound was my curiosity about a city in which music was not part of young people's everyday experience. In 2018, on the occasion of the centennial jubilee of the foundation of the orchestra, I challenged the institution with a vision: over the next 100 years at the very latest, every child in the city must be brought into contact with music. It should become routine. This provided a way for me to continue an old tradition. As early as 1918 the citizens of Cleveland supported their orchestra to broadcast the idea of classical music. I realise that this cultural aim will not solve any concrete problems, create a job for anyone unemployed or reform any criminal. But I believe that a city in which music is a matter of course and classical music is accessible to all is a place where there are inherently more opportunities. A city in which people listen more. A city in which the togetherness of an orchestra takes over the function of an example.

The famous basketball team the Cleveland Cavaliers has also demonstrated how splendid identification can be. In 2016 the team won the National Basketball Association Championship. The whole city was buzzing. And this in spite of a ticket for a game costing at least $350, a sum unattainable for many Clevelanders. Unfortunately the Cavaliers' success was not to last. After the sale of their star player

LeBron James, who now earns $35.65 million dollars per annum with the LA Lakers, things went downhill again – a setback from which the Cavaliers are still recovering today.

It is well known that sport and music have many things in common. For example, one 'plays' basketball just as one 'plays' the violin, oboe or piano – an aspect that I consider of vital importance when making music. The violin is not 'operated' or 'executed', it is played. As with sport, it is a question of playing, which gives pleasure only when it is taken seriously, when one cultivates it, when one practises, works on oneself, on one's own achievement – and that of the team.

I want music-making in Cleveland to become as natural as playing basketball, which is practised daily in suburban garage driveways and public places. I am concerned about a long-term investment both in the musical quality of the Cleveland Orchestra and its work in training and education. They should not be focused on a star – certainly not on me. My aim is, with the 100-year perspective that I sketched out in 2018, to develop the education programme to such a degree that it will long outlast the individual. And it makes me rather proud that we are well on the way to achieving this aim.

Admittedly I had much to learn, for example how insidiously the naturalness of culture can disappear and how quickly fundamental things can be abandoned. In the USA this process began about 40 years ago. At that time, more and more school bands were unceremoniously closed down to save expenses. This led to the fact that it is now significantly more difficult to find qualified wind players from the United States – a process that could also threaten Europe. We must be aware of the soil from which the next generations could grow. This is true above all of small bands, musical societies and churches. Otherwise, in Austria too, much that is typical of our tradition will be lost. In Cleveland I became aware that we are starting to feel the effects of a process that began a generation ago, and which cannot be reversed in a day. It is difficult to change the course of a strategy which has been followed for decades.

Franz Welser-Möst in his first season as music director
of the Cleveland Orchestra in 2002

And something else quickly became clear to me. Even a big institution such as an orchestra with its many musicians, its administration, sponsors, fans and extensive audience is not in a position to change an entire city on its own. It is always in danger of being self-referential, of addressing an audience which it is already reaching, and living within its own bubble. If one seriously wants to establish music as an everyday part of a whole city, one has to rely on the help of other institutions, such as businesses, schools, cultural and sport associations, and church communities.

So the first step was to realise that classical music, which I have always taken as a matter of course, has not been taken as a matter of course by the public for a long time. For this reason too, musical education must reach further than merely the availability of teaching. First of all, music must once again find its fixed place in the community. The basic question of education programmes is thus not what individual programmes one offers, but what is necessary to establish music once again as a crucial part of a community. All this will only work if the orchestra is understood as a model in its enterprise and business culture. In Cleveland we therefore want to be both regional and national pioneers, setting standards in orchestra management, not only accepting but also introducing changes, and at the same time always asking ourselves the question as to whether the path we have taken is the right one. It is and has always been our aim to play our part internationally in the premier league, when it is a question of orchestral and sound culture. But we have not forgotten that first and foremost we live in Cleveland, and that we take the role here of the regional provider of culture. We have come to understand that our local positioning is the nucleus of our national and international success.

Since I have been in Cleveland it has been important for me to take this cultural as well as social role seriously. The orchestra plays at schools on the West and East Side and cooperates intensively with the Metropolitan School District. It is our aim (with the help of a generous donation) to play in the presence of every student in the city. We are on good terms with the Cleveland Institute of Music as their partner, and are represented all over the city, for example with free concerts on the Day of Music, the Martin Luther King Concert and the open air performances on Independence Day. And as music director, it is also particularly important for me to support our own youth orchestra (COYO – The Cleveland Orchestra Youth Orchestra) with all the energy I possess.

All this has much to do with my musical education and the experiences of my youth. Today I realise that learning an instrument was probably a mark of distinction in a middle-class family in Wels as early as 1970. In a city like Cleveland it is impossible to ignore the fact that music does not form part of the everyday life of all people, but is the leisure activity of a largely privileged level of society. And that is exactly what I am not happy about. It is obvious that perhaps the most natural form of music-making – when a mother sings to her child in the evening – can have much to do with whether a musical institution exists in the city, which raises people's awareness of music.

How musical schooling can crash disastrously is something I had to learn with Sister Gerburga in Wels, and how music education can have an infectious effect was what I was able to experience later at the Musikgymnasium in Linz.

The passionate teacher: Balduin Sulzer

When my parents told me about the article on the new Musikgymnasium in Linz, I was enthusiastic. I still had to sit the entrance exams and musical audition for my new school, but I passed, and was able to begin my studies at the Musikgymnasium.

And there he was, this teacher with the long but sparse grey hairs on his semi-bald head. He was small, plump, always wore a sports jacket and entered the classroom in a dashing manner. He would shout 'Sit!' and bang his greasy old briefcase on the desk. Then he said: 'Anyone who is interested in what I am going to talk about, come to the front – the rest, sit at the back, and you will get low marks.' This unorthodox teacher was called Balduin Sulzer. He was a priest, a composer and an amateur critic on the popular newspaper *Kronen Zeitung*. When this man entered the classroom for the first time, it was as if a lightbulb went on in my head.. So, music education could be like this? And I, who had always been dreamy, began to blossom.

Shortly before Balduin Sulzer died, he gave an interview which I read with a chuckle. At the age of 87, he recalled his teaching style, which he described as follows: 'I don't know if I was an ideal teacher in accordance with the Federal Ministry. I did a great deal in an improvisatory manner, both in music and in other fields.' This was a huge understatement on his part. The Federal Ministry never interested him! He was a teacher with his own entirely anarchic plan.

We were at that time his experimental students: 21 young musical enthusiasts in the first year of the newly founded Musikgymnasium.

It was a joy to enter the school building each morning, which is now listed as a protected monument. It was built in the late Historicist style, and named after the Biedermeier poet Adalbert Stifter. Almost every day Balduin Sulzer surprised us with his passion. Teaching for him was not a theoretical matter; he understood the state-run curriculums at most as non-binding proposals. His teaching was pragmatic. He wanted to train musicians, so his first concern was that we should gain musical experience and understand the role that music plays in thinking. It was never a question of analysing and naming every single chord; it was important to him that we should sense and recognise the emotional effect of such a chord. During the first year, his listening exercises were feared, as were above all his rulings on rhythm, which for the first ten minutes of every lesson he rapped mercilessly on the desk with his car keys.

The founding of the Linz Musikgymnasium in 1974 was one of the lessons in matters of musical education in Upper Austria and proof that sometimes it takes only two people to move a mountain. One such, apart from Sulzer, was the director at the time of the Kremsmünster music school, Heinz Preiss. In 1973 he began to develop a musical concept for Upper Austria and constantly pestered a local government member with his visions. This man, who later became governor of Upper Austria, Josef Ratzenböck, was enthusiastic and became a Preiss sympathiser. The result was the foundation of the Linz Musikgymnasium, which was followed three years later, in 1977, by the foundation of the organisation of music schools in Upper Austria. Throughout the province, 34 music schools were founded to start with. The model was so successful that it was expanded. Today there are more than 150 music schools in operation – and demand is still higher than supply. A long-term and highly effective cultural basis for Upper Austria!

With Balduin Sulzer's teaching, everything was splendidly unorthodox. Here was a teacher who was himself passionately enthusiastic about what he was teaching us. His character made a lasting impression on me, showing that only those who are themselves enthusiastic can inspire the same in others. For a whole semester, Sulzer forgot to carry out class tests, which he found tedious, and then caught up with all of them in one go in the last week of term, with the comment: 'I already know who is good and who is not!' He repeatedly encouraged us to attend the concerts in the Brucknerhaus. At that time we had no money, so we had to be creative. One of us would buy a ticket, which we several times allowed to 'wander' outside, until in the end ten of us were sitting in the concert hall. Particularly popular were the guest performances by the Vienna Philharmonic. However, it was not long before our trick was discovered. The director, Karl Gerbel, had realised what we were up to. But instead of reprimanding us, he instructed his ushers not to look too closely in the cases of the students from the Musikgymnasium. A small gesture which, looking back, was an act of incredible generosity. Would something of the sort still be possible today?

Balduin Sulzer was in his 40s when he began to teach us. At the age of 17 he had joined the Cistercian order at Wilhering Abbey, and it was here that he took the religious name of Balduin (his original name was Josef). He studied theology and philosophy in Linz and Rome, and received his musical training at the Bruckner Conservatory in Linz, the Pontifical Institute for Church Music in Rome and the Vienna University of Music and Performing Arts. In 1955 he was ordained as a priest and initially taught at the Wilhering Abbey school. This account of his career alone shows how cosmopolitan my teacher was, a phenomenon that we as his students all admired.

At that time we lived like young dogs, roaming through the neighbourhood, debating and making music. When I sang my first *Messiah* as a bass in the choir of the Linz Chamber Orchestra under Sulzer, my knees knocked together during the *Hallelujah* Chorus.

It was the music teacher and composer Balduin Salzer who showed Franz Welser-Möst how passionately enthusiastic music could make people feel

And we also often appeared with the school orchestra, for example for regional businesses such as the VÖEST steelworks in Linz, where we played George Gershwin's *Rhapsody in Blue* to the workers. These experiences too were formative for me and have certainly influenced our education programme in Cleveland.

Not infrequently, after the concerts at the Brucknerhaus, our teacher invited us to a local hostelry. 'Come on, let's go and have a drink', was one of Balduin Sulzer's favourite phrases. And then we would go to the 'Breida', a small, cosy bar. Here Balduin would order apple juice for us all – and also beer when we were older. Generously, he also paid the bill. And we discussed what we had heard. With youthful arrogance, we dissected the failings of all, including the

Vienna Philharmonic, and had patent remedies ready. It was that time when we thought we knew better than anyone else.

My parents were pleased that their son had finally found a place where he was happy and contented. I remember that one morning, after an extended celebration with my friends, I was sneaking home. In the street I encountered my mother, who was just coming back from the baker's. 'What are you doing here?' she asked, and I answered: 'Going to get some sleep, before maybe going back to school.' My parents accepted all this. At our house there was only one red line as far as school was concerned, which could not be crossed: basically I had all the freedom I wanted; only having to repeat a year would not be tolerated. But luckily that did not happen.

At the school, Balduin Sulzer accurately recognised and encouraged our talents. At that time, in 1976, I was the section leader for the second violins in the small school orchestra. One day Balduin said to me in an offhand manner: 'Tomorrow you will take over the rehearsal.' So I suddenly found myself standing in front of my schoolmates and 'conducting', or doing what I thought was conducting.

Increasingly he handed over rehearsals to me, and I enjoyed it. About six months later I asked him if I might conduct a concert one day, and he thought there was no reason why not, if I organised everything myself. He then uttered the all-important sentence: 'Conducting begins with setting up the seats!' So I became my own impresario. I organised our first summer seminar in the summer of 1977 at Kremsmünster Abbey, where we all slept in the large dormitory of the hall of residence, raised funds, organised the transport of the instruments and musicians, had posters printed and was my own orchestra manager. In mid-August, after a week of rehearsals with my schoolmates, we were ready. We gave our first concert together at the Dunkelhof, a historic town house in Steyr. On the programme were Mozart's Divertimento K.137, Bach's Triple Concerto, a flute concerto by Antonio Vivaldi and Mozart's *Eine kleine Nachtmusik*.

Our parents came, and my father had brought some musician friends with him in his Citroen Dyane 6. And Balduin Sulzer was there too, and – I believe – proud of us.

That the first concert I conducted took place in the same town where I was to have played Schubert on that fateful day a good two years later is another strange coincidence. When I emerged from the silence after our accident, I wanted to get back to school as quickly as possible. For 12 weeks the whole of my upper body was encased in plaster, but I wanted to prove to myself that I could still play the violin. I did in fact continue to play, but my nerve-endings were too severely injured for a professional career.

From then on, Balduin Sulzer encouraged my career as a conductor, even after we had graduated as the first year of Linz Musikgymnasium students. The school orchestra was no longer an option for us alumni, and we had to start something new. So we founded the Jeunesse Orchestra Linz, which was from then on to become my great passion. In fact it was with this orchestra that I appeared for the first time in 1982, in the Great Hall of the Wiener Musikverein. When I was 20 years old, after a successful performance of Beethoven's Mass in C Major, Balduin suggested the *Missa solemnis* for the following year. To be honest, I felt both enormous fear and great respect for this gigantic work. 'What's your problem?' he asked. 'You are 20 years old and scared stiff. So what? Other people conduct it aged 50 – and they are scared stiff too. The difference is that you will then have been going around scared stiff for 30 years.' He laughed. So I summoned all my courage and conducted the *Missa solemnis*.

I learned many important things about music from Balduin Sulzer, including how inspiring music can be for people. From Linz I moved on to studying at the University of Music and Performing Arts in Munich. But much of what has made me into the musician I have become was learnt from Balduin Sulzer.

Is music really necessary?

One of my good friends is the singer Simon Keenlyside. When he became a father, we were sitting together, and at some point he said: 'Later my son will learn the piano.' I hesitated and then said: 'And what if he doesn't want to?' Simon looked at me, bewildered: 'Then of course I will force him.' When he saw that I was not convinced, he continued: 'We're forced by the school and the state to study mathematics. Why shouldn't we be allowed to make our children study what is important to us?' This was an opinion that made me think.

Simon's point of view is more understandable when one considers that, no matter where you look, music teaching has not for a long time been part of the everyday life of our schools. In 2017, in Germany's primary schools alone, 80 per cent of all music lessons have been dropped. The German Music Council justifiably calls it a scandal that the fourth richest industrial nation cannot manage to secure the musical education of its children. And we are speaking of the homeland of Bach, Brahms and Beethoven. But at least as bad is the fact that music is no longer regarded even as a secondary subject, and some politicians – even with reference to university education – assert that only mathematics, physics, economics and law are fields in which one can remain internationally competitive today.

The access of various countries to music education is something I will discuss separately later, but will say just this now: nations such as Finland, where music and art have as much status as mathematics or chemistry, perform best by far in the international PISA (Programme for International Student Assessment) studies. And in scientific terms there is no longer any doubt that musical encouragement has a direct influence on the brain development of babies, small children and young people, particularly since our neuronal structures continue to be developed up to the age of 25.

During this period it is above all a question of the links known as the synapses. They ensure that our brain becomes more efficient and creative. Here, making music can play a decisive role. I like

Rehearsals in the Abbot's room at Kremsmünster Abbey for the first concert (1977) conducted by Franz Welser-Möst

what Gerald Hüther, the neurobiologist from Göttingen, says when he describes the connection between evolution and music: 'It is strange, but in neuroscientific terms there is every indication that the most useless achievement of which humans are capable – and that is undoubtedly carefree, purposeless singing – has the most useful effect on the development of children's brains.'

One of the most prominent researchers into the human brain, the neuroscientist Wolf Singer, has a similar view. He has observed that our sensory organs are so arranged that they need to exploit only a fraction of their possibilities to create what we perceive as 'reality'. Basically our brain is constantly trying to make sense of everything that surrounds us. To do this, the individual cells link together and find a meaningful form even in the aleatory music of a John Cage, that is, in compositions in which accident plays an important part.

The great question is where the brain gets its criteria of order. Brain research distinguishes various forms of the acquisition of knowledge. One is foreknowledge, an implicit knowledge, which, through the connectivity of our nerve cells, is already present before our birth through the evolution process and is genetically inherited. Another form of gaining knowledge takes place starting from birth; this process is partly implicit, so happens unconsciously. And then we also acquire knowledge through conscious study, whether in everyday life, in the kindergarten or at school.

The assumption that there is a brain centre in which the 'I' is housed and in which 'reality' is put together is wrong. In fact, our brain works as a distributive system with very flat organisational structures. In other words, many brain areas work on many sensory impressions at the same time and transform them in many different places into emotions and information, from which we construct our perception and consider our actions. The task of art in this process, Wolf Singer explains, is to confront our brain with the unknown: images that play with our perception, poems which reveal their meaning only between the lines, or music which is able to create emotions through sound. Art can activate our brain in another way than does the reality of the world. In doing so, it stimulates us to create entirely new synapses and open more windows in our brain.

Making music demands a particularly complex interplay of quite different abilities. It builds on the hearing, vision, touch and fine motor skills. Just imagine the control functions that are needed for a stroke of the violin bow: the recognition and reading of the notes, the conversion of what is seen into different movements of the right and left hand, together with the simultaneous listening and the matching of the sound produced to the expectations developed in the brain, then perhaps also the emotional characterisation of the sound as cheerful or sad music. Scientific research has found that in the processing of music, even the Broca area takes part, one of the two language centres.

All this affects our cognitive and emotional development. Music may not make us cleverer, but, particularly in the early childhood phase, it supports the linking of our synapses and with it the possibilities and flexibility of our brain. It promotes mathematical understanding and reading comprehension at the same time. It concurrently stimulates movement and rhythm, discipline and an understanding of give and take. But the most important aspect for me is that making music above all cultivates those abilities which I perceive as particularly deficient: music encourages interaction, listening, the sense of community, and empathy. All these are effects of learning, which are not consciously perceived, but simply 'happen' while one makes music.

With all these realisations, Simon Keenlyside's question should certainly be allowed. Why do we force our children to learn writing, reading and mathematics, but shut our eyes to musical education? How can it be that we simply ignore the findings of brain research? How can we treat the education, development and training of our children so irresponsibly?

Meanwhile, the fact that music teaching simply no longer takes place at many schools is balanced by the increasingly high expectations placed on the orchestras in question. As the schools give up, orchestras are expected to take on musical training. One may deplore it, but one can't ignore such a responsibility. The time when the only concerns of a chief conductor were the repertoire, rehearsals and performances is long over. We now need to bear in mind the social potential of an orchestra. And we must consider carefully what object an orchestra's music teaching can and should fulfil.

My fundamental notion is that all music for a start represents a form: rhythm, note values and harmonic rules define a frame. This is as true of major-minor tonality as it is of the serialism of Neue Musik. Even music which consciously wishes to be formless cannot do without form – if only to break it. With this in mind, I understand music as order which makes our orientation easier and defines our space and time. Perhaps this is exactly what we often lack today: a form or frame which helps us to locate our own position in the world. I firmly believe that freedom is possible only within a structure of order.

For the same reason, a very simple rule takes priority over our diverse activities in Cleveland: The stage is sacred! This means that music is taken seriously on the podium, both by us, the musicians, and also by the young people. For whoever believes that music can help people in their orientation is well advised to take it seriously.

In the Cleveland Youth Orchestra I made the acquaintance of a young man who explained to me how important the discipline of practice had been for him personally. He comes from a difficult background; his father is in prison and his mother is an alcoholic. He told me that the violin had been his salvation. He had fallen in love with the instrument and spent hours learning to play it. Practising had structured his day, spurred him on and made him ambitious. Meanwhile he plays together with other young people and his dearest wish is to become a professional musician.

I tell this story because it shows that we should take musical education seriously – because young people also want to take music seriously! It may be that music has become a minor matter in many schools; it is all the more important that orchestras provide advocacy for the value of music. As music director of the Vienna State Opera I was already concerned that operas for children were tucked out of sight in the basement or in the attic. It is precisely on children that the main auditorium makes the greatest impression. And this is what the first contact with music must be about: making an impression. The same, by the way, is true of the sound. Why are so many recordings of 'music for children' made with – if I may say so – mediocre orchestras? If we want to infuse young people with enthusiasm for our art, it is positively essential that we give them the best we have to offer.

This is why it is important to me that education does not deteriorate into an irritating minor issue for an orchestra. Work on perfection in sound must be the central concern. Only an orchestra which can create great moments in the evening will succeed in the long term in convincing young people. In other words: it would be wrong to use educational work to polish the image of an orchestra. It would be fatal to neglect work on the sound in favour of work on education. Education must become a matter of course for a leading orchestra – as much so as striving after the ideal sound at every evening performance.

Our concept in Cleveland consists not in forcing every child to make music, but to show every child how beautiful it can be to do so. We have made a conscious decision to adopt a two-pronged approach. On the one hand it is a question of the broad impact of music, of establishing classical music as the norm in public life, and on the other to encourage top talent. To this end, a special programme for highly talented musicians – often from deprived backgrounds – is in development.

As an Austrian, I like to compare this balancing act with skiing. A Marcel Hirscher (regarded as probably the greatest skier in Alpine history) in Austria was possible only because skiing is a mass sport with us, and there are many role models. At the same time, however, talents such as Hirscher's must also be intensively and personally nourished. It is only through this that well-trained competitive sportspeople can go on to inspire a new generation of young people. The same is true of musicians.

In this chapter, we have been considering the question of whether music is really necessary. I agree with my friend Simon Keenlyside. If we think that mathematics and physics are necessary, we should also include music in the canon of those fields that we consider vitally important. We cannot and should not any longer ignore the findings of brain research. Our young people have a right to music. And furthermore, if we have the opportunity to encourage a love of music in others, instead of forcing it on them, then we will have achieved the aim which is at the core of my deepest convictions.

The first silence

At that time there were no coffins for children, so the funeral director came into our living room with a cardboard box under his arm. He had come to collect my sister. He placed Veronika into the container and simply took her away with him. Veronika had died at eight months old. I was four at the time. When I recall this moment today, I still see it all from a child's perspective. Everything was so big: the funeral director in his black suit, my parents beside him. It is disturbing for a child to see his parents looking so helpless, confronted with something too big for them, too big for anyone. The death of a child is too big for all of us. It was the first time that I realised that even for my parents there were things they could not control. And it was the first time I heard the silence – a raging silence.

Since Veronika had been born in 1964, the youngest of six siblings, it had become quieter in our house. She was born with a heart defect and Down syndrome. Very rapidly it became clear to all of us in the family that she was not going to win the battle to stay with us, that sooner or later we would lose her. And so the time during which Veronika was with us was a muted time. Everything revolved around her, our hopes, our fears, our days and nights. A time like that unites a family.

On the day when the black-suited funeral director with the cardboard box rand our doorbell, the decrescendo had finally entered the silence. Time stood still. The world stopped turning. But the reassuring feeling that filled me 14 years later, when our car came off the road, did not present itself that day. This silence was surrounded by an emptiness – by nothing.

A few days later our family was standing in the cemetery – my parents, hand in hand, behind them my siblings and myself. We were saying goodbye to Veronika.

I believe that with her death, something happened to each of us. Particularly my mother – she who was so deeply devout, and who now had to experience her own daughter being taken away by God.

The roles at home were divided up in such a way that my father was the one who sometimes reacted with fits of temper and could fly into a rage over a triviality. My mother was different; nothing could disturb her calm. Whatever we did, whatever happened, she relied on her faith and radiated contentment. And this did not change after Veronika's death.

As a child I had already realised that faith was no guarantee of mental balance. My father's mother was at least as devout as my own mother and went to church every day. Nevertheless she feared death and during her last days she had the delusion that the devil was standing outside her door. She died when I was 13 years old.

Veronika's illness and early death left their mark on my mother. When my father was finally appointed medical officer in the nearby city of Eferding, and came home every day and not only every other weekend, our family situation began to ease. Now my mother finally had time to express herself fully. She became interested in politics, stood as a candidate for the Austrian People's Party (Österreichische Volkspartei, ÖVP), and was elected to the National Assembly. From 1979 to 1986 she was the first woman to represent the state of Upper Austria in Vienna. Her political philosophy was thoroughly progressive from a present-day point of view. On the one hand she was deeply religious and as a result conservative, and on the other, her faith gave her a strong concern for the world. The best term to describe my mother is probably Christian Socialist. For example, she founded an association for unmarried mothers in Wels. Her political work was also influenced by her private experiences. I believe that Veronika's death, perhaps subconsciously, constituted a large part of my mother's agenda. She actively championed the rights of disabled people, and it was not until her funeral in 2014 that I learned that the dropped pavement kerbs in Austria, which assist people with mobility problems, are the result of her initiative. She also had a street named after her in her native city.

The twins Franz
and Elisabeth in the
arms of their parents
surrounded by their
older siblings

A liberal atmosphere also prevailed in our house. I have already
mentioned that only a few red lines existed in our family. Within these
limits we could express ourselves with complete freedom. My mother
encouraged us children in whatever we aspired to. Today the little
story that we siblings like to tell each other may seem obvious, but
in the 1960s it was not so. When my sister Maria was two and a half
years old and wanted to set the table with our best china, there was
no question that my mother would allow her to do it. And indeed,
nothing was broken. That was how my mother was; she gave us
responsibility early on, and showed us that she trusted us.

Even when, after my accident, I began to quarrel with the faith
that was so important to her, when I cast doubt on God, seeking
enlightenment in philosophy and alternative religion, she never
criticized me. She never let me feel that she had anything against
what I was looking for. In this respect my mother was indeed liberal.

The car accident, my teachers August Patzel and Balduin Sulzer,
but above all my parents – often one learns only later in life how

one has become the person one is. What I know today is that I was incredibly lucky to have been surrounded in my youth by people who helped me to develop and express what inspires and really touches me: music. It is this experience that has become the key to musical experience for me, and to that for which I strive as a musician: self-reliance and freedom as the greatest gifts given to the individual and the basis of one's creativity.

Music against a noisy world

When education is discussed, one hears from the mouths of many politicians that the schools are missing their target market. For me, this has the unpleasant aftertaste of pressure – the pressure to conform to the speed of the market, the pressure to weigh up the relevance, usefulness and practice orientation of knowledge, the pressure towards bite-sized portion control of quickly produced and easily disposable morsels of knowledge. After all, the creativity which everyone, absolutely everyone, needs in every area of life lies in the freedom and self-knowledge of the individual. It means not only the exploitation of one's own potential, but also self-motivation. Only then can it provide the expected energy boost for a community, an institution, a society. The original meaning of the word school (from ancient Greek *scholé*, Latin *schola*) is a place of leisure, of rest, of pausing for thought. Here the places of education, art and music meet. It is a question of a sphere of freedom for creativity, in which individuals confront traditions, develop innovative ideas, recognise connections and construct a future with team spirit. The idea of freedom as an indispensable condition for (self-)education and the formation of the individual, for maturity and self-assurance in the encounter and debate with the collective, is a profoundly humanistic concern and has always characterised European cultural and intellectual history. In this way, for example, in Greek classical antiquity the *septem artes liberales* formed the canon of studies. These seven liberal arts consisted of the *trivium* of the subjects based on language and logical argument – grammar, rhetoric and dialectic – and the *quadrivium*, subdivided into arithmetic, geometry, music (!) and astronomy. The free arts were named as such to distinguish them from the practical arts, because – as Seneca puts it in his 88th Epistle – they are 'worthy of a free person'. Education, art, and above all music as a basis for the free individual – a profoundly European value!

Probably one of the most famous pieces of writing on the connection between education and aesthetics is Friedrich Schiller's On the *Aesthetic Education of Man* (1795), in which he reflects in 27 letters on beauty (by which he means aesthetics) as a foundation stone of the human community – and of a state. In the sixth letter he laments that man is becoming an 'impress' of his 'craft' on the one hand and his 'science' on the other. The abstract thinker has a 'cold heart', the businessman a 'narrow heart'. Schiller comes to the conclusion that there is 'no other way to make a reasonable being out of a sensuous man than by making him first aesthetic'. The conductor Bruno Walter, whom I greatly revere, in an interview towards the end of his life, expressed it in this way: 'You have to have maturity to understand beauty.'

I find it fascinating that at present cultures which we credit with a particularly radical emphasis on rapid growth, expansion, pressure to achieve and competitiveness, have long ago discovered for themselves virtues which were originally at home with us in Europe. China is the best example of this.

A pianist such as Lang Lang, whom I have known since he was 16 years old and with whom I am on friendly terms, is a pop star in his own country. He has more than 11 million followers on different social media platforms, and the image that he likes to promote of himself is that of the trendily dressed young man who presents himself at the heart of old Europe, as at his wedding, which he celebrated at the palace of Versailles. When I asked him who followed him in his social media platforms and what reactions he was getting, Lang Lang

With the pianist Lang Lang after a public rehearsal with the Vienna Philharmonic in Tianjin, China, in November 2018

answered that his followers were for the most part parents – mothers and fathers who hoped that their children would be as successful in music as he.

Is it not astonishing that classical music has taken over that role in China that it perhaps played most recently with us in the 1960s and 1970s – a symbol of the rise of a new civil society and a successful, open-minded social group? About 50 years ago, classical music had a similar impact in Japan, when that country was celebrating its economic miracle.

China has one of the biggest music support programmes worldwide. I will gladly admit that a different approach to music education exists in Asia from that in liberal Finland, and it is certainly also worthy of discussion whether Chinese education methods correspond to our ideals. What I find more interesting is the basic question of why a nation like China lays such massive importance on music. President Xi Jinping announces publicly that he encourages the development of music schools because learning an instrument enhances the creativity and thus the efficiency of the people. In other words, music teaching is a national objective. No one in China's political leadership ranks believes that children who have received an education in music are 'missing their target market'. On the contrary, the secondary knowledge of music education – creativity and flexibility – is for Chinese politics a value in itself, which will also serve economic productivity and thus worldwide leadership in many areas. When I work with Chinese students or musicians, I also find that they are influenced by the progressive values of classical music, by cosmopolitanism, the desire for freedom and individuality. The Chinese conductor Long Yu, who incidentally was trained in Berlin, and now directs the China Philharmonic Orchestra, says: 'The development of China should take place according to the laws of art, intelligent, free and oriented towards the criteria of quality.'

I ask myself why China of all nations relies on music education while we in Europe, that continent which practically invented classical music, is threatened with losing the value of our own tradition.

If we continue our world journey into the USA, we see a different picture. Classical music has always been a niche here, even more so than in Europe. Over the years it became increasingly my aim to make classical music accessible to every young person in Cleveland, admittedly a very ambitious plan. In contrast to Europe, in the American system the cultural field is left to be dealt with by private initiatives. Classical music thus only becomes important when the people of a city are interested in it. This means furthermore that cultural institutions and creative artists repeatedly have to give proof of their relevance. Even institutions such as the Metropolitan Opera and Carnegie Hall in the USA have not for a long time had any inherent right to survive.

The advantage of American cultural politics is that the public sector has only very limited influence on local cultural structures. The social opportunities open to an orchestra in America are not determined in Washington, but on the spot and to a great extent by the orchestra itself. Before I took on the post in Cleveland, I was given decisive advice by the experienced music manager Tom Morris – he was artistic director in Cleveland and Boston: 'Have a look at the board.' What he meant was that the most important thing for an orchestra is the top management. If they were ready to move mountains, then one would be able to move mountains – no matter what administration was in power and who was president. Luckily, the Board of the Cleveland Orchestra did and does want to move mountains.

So it can be an advantage that a cultural structure such as an orchestra depends not only on government benevolence but also on private sponsorship. Later I will have something to say about the structures of various cultural institutions, but here will say only this: any system is only as good as the way it is operated, and every system has advantages and disadvantages. The fact is that even in the USA the state subsidises culture – not directly, that is, but because taxpayers can set financial donations to an institution such as the Cleveland Orchestra against their tax bill. This means that which institutions are supported depends on the supporters themselves, and not on the government. Thus, for example, we have received from the Maltz Family Foundation in Cleveland a donation of more than 20 million dollars, which we were able to use to enable young people to attend concerts.

In the last 20 to 30 years, populist tendencies have become increasingly louder and stronger, and not only in politics. Simple messages are cobbled together and distributed with as thick a cudgel as possible. The image of an enemy is always part of this.

This means that culture which diversifies, and probes deeply into the complex individual that is man, has a very hard time. And the same is true of art. The deep experience of art that ideally allows us to discern the essential core of humanity stands in irreconcilable contrast to the ballyhoo of populism. Here I am referring to artistic experiences of quite different natures. It can for example be experienced in front of Tintoretto's *Crucifixion* in the Scuola Grande di San Rocco in Venice, which draws one into its complex cosmos of emotions. Or it can be released by a poem by Joseph von Eichendorff, which takes us by the hand with all its delicate ramifications, gives us wings and leads us to a lyrical and fragile place. Or think of Joseph Haydn's oratorio *The Seasons*, which tells the story of a human life with both humour and profundity, and fills our hearts with sunbeams. One could name so many more examples of uplifting and stirring experiences in art.

But let us see what status is given to art in our world of today. I have already discussed music education and its erosion, and we will later turn our attention to the abolition and merging of radio orchestras, while the closures of city theatres and opera houses has long been a reality. The cultural landscape built up over centuries is crumbling to such a massive extent that some insiders are even envisaging the permanent closure of the Met as a possibility. Can anyone still remember the New York City Opera? Was there an outcry about its closure at the time?

In Austria, too, since the 1990s an increasing indifference has been observed on the part of politicians as well as public opinion and even the cultural institutions, which seem only to be concerned about themselves. That in my own home of Upper Austria there are more than 50,000 music students, but the Brucknerhaus in Linz is struggling for its audience and its own survival, leaves me bewildered.

Differentiated listening and engaging with each other is not made easier for us by the general acoustic pollution. As early as Monday morning on any given week, there are loud announcements from the various entertainment and pop stations that there are only five days left to the weekend: party! It seems that in this over-loud, even distorted world we are engulfed by a higgledy-piggledy mentality of partying presumption – often transmitted via the flood of media images. It's about consumption, superficiality and as much leisure time as possible. The connection between a partying society and the noise of this world is striking. A partying society is not a quiet one, but a loud, decibelised one which cannot do without noise.

I remember a conversation with a young man, in his early 30s, who, when I asked him what his aims in life were, replied: 'Having fun!' This started a discussion between us about the concepts of 'fun' and 'pleasure'. Fun means enjoyment, entertainment, amusement; pleasure on the other hand means high spirits, a feeling of happiness, inner cheerfulness. Fun is what one has; pleasure is what one feels. Fun is the fulfilment of a hedonistic feeling, pleasure is a feeling created from deep within. Fun is associated with the outer, strident, active; pleasure with the inner, calm and contemplative. Fun is superficial and (self-)stupefying; pleasure is most enjoyable when it can be shared.

To my eyes, the concept of fun brings up images from television of the Ballermann beach restaurant in Mallorca; when I think of pleasure, I see before me, for example, young orchestral musicians in Cleveland, whom I have recruited and who are developing in a wonderful way. All of this may have its place in life; one does not exclude the other, but to devote one's life entirely to fun would mean an impoverishment for me.

I must confess that I sometimes feel like a stranger in this loud and euphoric world, in which so much is dealt with on the surface and so little in depth. And I see a frightening number of parallels between society and the musical landscape – whether it is orchestras that are calling for a Messiah, a saviour or a leader, instead of working long-term with a conductor towards a common future; whether it is music students and young artists who no longer ask what Beethoven's manuscripts look like, but how they themselves can sound different from all other interpreters of Beethoven before them; how they can get attention and make their mark. And one other thing unites politics and music: both seem no longer to have much grasp of the reality of people's lives. Politicians who explain complex situations, who place importance on nuances and think about them, hardly make an impact any more on our loud and overwrought world.

I am firmly of the opinion that orchestras can make their contribution, that music is again part of the self-understanding of many people. Music as a form that gives us orientation, music as potential order, music as depth in a life beyond a surface that is rushing away from us, music as a place of community and listening, music as an expression of quiet and pausing for thought, music as a calm anchor in a restless world. I know that I am not alone in my longing for silence. It is all the more important to find partners, sympathisers, people who work together for the art of music, who anchor it in the everyday, and musicians for whom every concert is always also a plea that we utter together against decibelisation and the noise of the world.

First journey

Meditative silence

Pain is a terrible thing. Perhaps the best comparison is with persistent intensity of sound, with uncontrolled noise beyond all structure: an acoustic chaos, to which one is helplessly subjected.

It was painful to learn that after my car accident the nerve fibres of my fingers had never healed to the point where I would be able to play the violin again to a professional standard. But I was also afflicted by totally tangible, physical pain, particularly in the form of dreadful back pain. After my time spent in the intensive care unit, then the general ward, with the whole upper part of my body in plaster for twelve weeks, I was regularly and continually plagued by pain – to an extent where I could no longer ignore it. I tried to reduce it a little with medications. Sometimes this helped, and sometimes it made it worse.

In the early 1990s, when I had met an osteopath, there was a gradual improvement. During my first year in Cleveland my wife suggested that I should myself take control of the battle against the noise of my pain. 'But how?' I asked. 'Well, with yoga perhaps,' she replied. So I looked for a yoga teacher, and very soon it became clear to me that this form of movement was about much more than simply the control of one's own body. In fact, yoga is based on the same principle as music, on the interplay between tension and release. In music, this balance represents probably the greatest art, and no composer has practised the interplay of tension and release as intensively as Richard Wagner in his opera *Tristan and Isolde*. For five hours he makes the audience wait for the releasing chord (of love). He repeatedly makes use of the so-called Tristan chord, which builds up the harmonic tension and then consoles us with the resolution the next time it resounds. An endless playing with our expectations, with our (listening) habits, and a musical challenge not to trust the familiar, but to think unconventionally.

My experience with yoga has been similar. Through the spiritual quests of my late youth I had already encountered various forms of meditation. With yoga it is also a question of using the body as a possibility for discovering totally new worlds. With me, this kind of contemplation usually leads to a sense of expanse, to a kind of inner experience of nature. When I practise yoga, there is a chance for that space of silence to open up that I experienced just before the car came off the road – that silence which appears in the perfect interplay of tension and release, and which I also enjoy in music.

Meanwhile, I have even developed the habit of regularly applying the brakes on my life as a musician, in order to gain release from tension. Thus, every year I withdraw for a while to take an F. X. Mayr course of treatment, to purge and detoxify my body – but also my spirit. This too is a form of silence.

Fasting saps one's energy. At such times I do not impose on myself a ban on studying a score, but last time I was forced to realise that the spiritual and physical potential of a fasting body can be overstretched if, during the treatment, I attempt once again to study the score for Richard Strauss's *Elektra*. But it is precisely such realisations that are for me the reason for these 'retreats': to shut the body down, to become humble – to be silent and withdraw.

Since I have been practising yoga, my back pains have almost completely disappeared. The noise of pain is no longer my ever-present companion. Yoga has given me the opportunity no longer to remain trapped in objective thinking. The physically tangible, to which many limits are usually set, dissolves. Yoga can lead to a state similar to the one I experience when I am 'in music'. Here too, by means of physical work, the physicality of making music creates an acoustic space whose special nature lies in its abstraction, in the dematerialisation of the concrete – in an endless expanse.

II.

The places of music

On the organisation of sound

My years of apprenticeship in London

The steep and stony path of my career began in August 1990 in the plush lobby of the Hotel Bristol in Salzburg, and dropped me, quite unawares, onto a rocky road of apprenticeship. The director of the London Philharmonic Orchestra asked me: 'What do you think, Herr Welser-Möst, do you want to be in charge of our orchestra from September?'

One has to bear in mind that Sir Thomas Beecham had founded the celebrated orchestra in 1932; Klaus Tennstedt took it over from Sir Georg Solti in 1983. Tennstedt's health, however, had for some time not been cooperating, and two years earlier he had made the surprising announcement of his retirement. Negotiations for his replacement took place with Daniel Barenboim and Riccardo Muti – but nothing happened. Now, suddenly, I was faced with someone sitting opposite me, a 30-year-old newcomer, currently working in Winterthur and Lausanne and running the orchestra in Norrköping, Sweden, and asking me if I would take over this job.

I did not think about it for long – and that was a mistake. I did not even ask myself why I, a greenhorn, was being made this offer. I simply thought 'Madness!', without suspecting that my 'yes' would be the beginning of a six-year odyssey of misunderstandings, insults, intrigues and catastrophes, a resounding failure – now it can be said. My time in London was probably the most painful of my life as a conductor, and at the same time the most instructive in all the non-musical areas of our occupation.

As a student I had lived in London twice, in 1980 and 1981. Both visits were incredibly enlightening for me. I had come from tranquil Linz, where as late as 1977 people left the concert hall in protest during a performance of *Le Sacre du Printemps*. Igor Stravinsky was still considered a revolutionary by us. More than 60 years earlier, on 29 May 1913, the work had caused a scandal on many levels at the Théâtre des Champs-Élysées. Never before had an audience heard such radical music, the choreography of Vaslav Nijinsky was considered outrageous, and the musicians faced entirely new technical challenges. All this led to tumult and physical altercations in the aisles, fist-fights and throwing of chairs. At the end of it the police recorded 27 injuries.

In the early 1980s the mood in the British capital was quite different from that in Linz. Here I suddenly discovered a sold-out programme with works by Stravinsky, and an attentive and enthusiastic audience. I heard Sir Georg Solti and the London Symphony Orchestra, and visited the English National Opera and the Royal Opera House in Covent Garden, where Sir Colin Davis was principal conductor. I was there when Gilbert Kaplan, the American entrepreneur and amateur conductor with an obsession with Gustav Mahler, performed the Symphony No. 2 with the London Symphony Orchestra – his version was chosen as the recording of the year by the *New York Times*. It was in England that I first heard a work of Leoš Janáček, performed by the Welsh National Opera, and was totally overwhelmed and captivated by this music. New horizons opened up for me at that time, and the little money that I had at my disposal as a student was spent in its entirety on opera and concert tickets. During my stays in London I lived mostly on toast and marmalade, and when I came back to Wels for Christmas in 1981, my mother was somewhat shocked: I was even more slender than before and had lost seven kilos. In compensation I had enriched myself with a massive amount of music.

Before being offered the job in London barely ten years later, I had already had early musical encounters with the London Philharmonic Orchestra. For example, in 1986 the British agent

Martin Campbell-White telephoned me to ask if I, as understudy to Jesús López Cobos, would conduct Mozart's Haffner Symphony and his Requiem – with the wonderful Felicity Lott. Again I did not hesitate for a second, boarded a flight next day, landed in London about 12pm and by 2pm was standing in front of the orchestra. After three rehearsals the performance took place, and one reviewer wrote that I would be walking in the footsteps of Karl Böhm – a *succès d'estime* which did not yet allow me to surmise what one must be ready to expect if the mood of the British press suddenly changes.

In 1988 the orchestra was planning a tour, and I was to stand in as replacement conductor for Klaus Tennstedt, who was already very ill by then, and Mariss Jansons. As it turned out, both had to cancel their concerts, one just after the other, and I took over. On one of the programmes was Sibelius' Symphony No. 1 and Tchaikovsky's Symphony No. 5, and on the other Beethoven's Sixth and Mahler's Fourth, again with Felicity Lott, alternating with Beethoven's *Eroica*. It was a remarkable tour. We gave guest performances at all the great concert houses in Europe, including the Concertgebouw in Amsterdam and – unforgettably for me – the Vienna Musikverein, whose unique atmosphere I had already been able to experience when I appeared with the Jeunesse Orchestra from Linz. Of course, on that occasion many of my friends and families were sitting in the stalls. For a young musician like myself this was an incredible honour.

So now, in 1990, I was to succeed Klaus Tennstedt and I said 'yes'. What at the time I did not take into account were the battle lines that were drawn up behind the scenes. Probably even Winston Churchill would have been proud of the tactical games of the British classical music scene at the time. In the first place it was a question of the residency of the London Philharmonic Orchestra at the Royal Festival Hall, which had been put out to tender by the Southbank Centre. The second orchestra in the running for this position was the Philharmonia Orchestra London. In the invitation to tender, a number of concessions to the management of the Southbank were demanded, and a principal conductor was sought who would be vested with great authority. What I did not suspect was that I had been asked partly because it was assumed that a younger and relatively inexperienced conductor would be malleable and less self-assertive. They thought: 'Let's get Welser-Möst; he will be happy to be here, and we can use him in any way we like.' I however came to the Thames with a suitcase full of visions. Among other things, I envisaged a concert hall in which we could be 100 per cent our own bosses. At the time there was an opportunity to acquire the Battersea Power Station on the Thames with a pocket of land attached, for a pound. When I put forward this suggestion to our supervisory board, they laughed at me, with the remark that I was simply not an Englishman and would not understand certain circumstances. This was not going to go well for long.

For reasons of the orchestra's prestige, I was initially installed in the Savoy Hotel. I lived there up to Black Wednesday in 1992, with its associated escalation of the financial crisis. Overnight the pound had suddenly diminished in value by 25 per cent. Because of the cash flow problems, I received no salary for eight months, and a significantly less costly accommodation was sought for me. Its financial straits were part of the orchestra's basic problems.

It was not long before British critics gave me the unflattering nickname 'Frankly Worse than Most' (a play on my name). Today I can chuckle about it, but at the time I did not feel like laughing. It was the first time I had been faced with this sort of direct criticism, without knowing exactly what was behind it. Was it really my performance as conductor and artistic director? Was it the continuing trench warfare? I was unable to evaluate all this, and only sensed that I personally was being used as a buffer by several interested parties. The low blows became more and more powerful, while support from the orchestra became ever weaker.

It is important to understand that the London Philharmonic Orchestra was at that time also going through a phase of extensive restructuring. It was not until 1985 that the self-administration introduced in 1939 had been abandoned and John Willan, a financial expert and graduate of the Royal Academy of Music, had been appointed as manager. Willan had previously been a successful producer at the record company EMI. And my time in London was also marked by a number of recordings for the label, with which I had an exclusive contract. We recorded works by Mendelssohn and Stravinsky among others, but also by Franz Schmidt, the composer born in 1874 in Bratislava and much too rarely performed.

In the end, the London Philharmonic Orchestra actually became the resident orchestra at the Royal Festival Hall. Whether in Vienna or in Cleveland, it was always clear that a concert hall and its acoustics contributed significantly to the sound of an orchestra. This however also meant that the management of the Southbank Centre could exert an influence on our programme. And so, as a result of partly crippling and protracted discussions, works were put on the programme which gained the Southbank Centre a certain degree of media attention, but had a negative effect on our box office. How good it would have been to be really the masters in our own house!

In 1993 the big question was also asked in public. After the financial crisis, politicians and press were discussing the setting up of a London super-orchestra at the expense of the existing companies. The so-called Arts Council admittedly agreed to retain the status quo. As a result, the London Philharmonic Orchestra and the Philharmonia Orchestra London, at the time directed by Giuseppe Sinopoli, made peace with each other and from then on shared the residency at the Royal Festival Hall. Since I personally continued to be in the line of fire, in February 1994 I offered my resignation to the board of directors, which consisted mainly of musicians. The absurd thing was that, while the press and orchestra liked to use me as a doormat for their sensitivities, they had little interest in letting me go. My resignation was declined. So I stayed, more out of a sense of duty than enthusiasm.

A few days after my resignation offer, I decided to clear off, drove to the seaside and went for a walk along the beach at Bournemouth. This was where Sir Thomas Beecham had taken time off from his stressful life in London. During those days I walked for miles and miles by the sea, the wind whipping against my face. Had I really perhaps chosen the wrong profession? Were my critics right after all? Was I not born to be a conductor? In any case I was unhappy, and, yes, even despairing. Perhaps I should do something completely different. I called my American manager Edna Landau and told her I wanted to call it a day in London. I said that I would even consider abandoning music altogether. She listened patiently and then replied in her wonderfully laconic way: 'Oh, Franz, just stop walking along the beach!' But my thoughts were continuing to circle, and some time later I asked my wife: 'Would you still love me if I wasn't a principal conductor any more?'

I continued to fulfil my contract in London up to 1996, at the same time not looking for a new position. After I left, the *Guardian* wrote about 'unlovely years' in which the 'high hopes' that had been placed in me had 'somehow not been fulfilled'. Another newspaper, less stylishly, summed up: 'He came from nowhere, he is going nowhere.' I would be lying if I said that such phrases, whether justified or not, did not hurt.

In our world, failure is rarely a subject for discussion. Conductors are simply silently dropped. But with the passing of time, failure begins to become understandable. Many things have become clearer to me. The basic constellation in London was from the first day catastrophic; the various expectations of the orchestra, management, press, public and myself put me in an impossible position from the start. And of course, through lack of experience of the highly charged cultural situation in the vibrant metropolis of London, I also personally made many mistakes. As unlovely as all this was, as painful and frustrating, I ultimately have much for which to thank my time in London. What I had learned was that dreams and visions can be realised only if the structures are appropriate and the environment is the right one.

It was now clear to me what I absolutely had to be aware of, if an orchestra was ever to offer me another post. From then on I never accepted a job only on the basis of a flattering offer. I would not agree without taking a careful look at the challenges that such a task would bring with it. I was no longer interested in any offers where I did not sense that the institution and myself could perhaps develop a common vision. And I learned one other thing at the end of my time in London: that I was prepared to let go. That a resignation represented for me not an empty threat, but a genuine possibility.

Today I am at peace with London, and often meet with people from that time. And the city too welcomes me with an open heart when, for example, I visit as conductor with the Cleveland Orchestra. When I left London, I was full of self-doubt, so much so that I was inwardly ready to give up conducting altogether. I considered going back to university to study law. I was not yet sure what course of study to decide for, when a telephone call interrupted my deliberations. The artistic director of the Zurich Opera, Alexander Pereira, was inviting me to come to his house.

Very grand opera in Zurich

In Zurich, too, I was greeted by public opinion with its irresistible directness. The Swiss press received me not only as the new principal conductor of the Zurich Opera House, but also as the 'loser from London'.

For myself, I identified Zurich as my last chance. If it doesn't work here either, I told myself, I will look for a new profession. In the end, I stayed in Switzerland for 13 years, and – I can say this today – grew every year along with the house and the company. I could learn the lessons of London only after my time in England, because I was too inexperienced then and the conditions on the spot had demanded too much of me. I first had to admit that I had failed before I could learn from this failure. In Zurich, things looked quite

Alexander Pereira and Franz Welser-Möst worked together for 13 years
as artistic director and principal conductor at the Zurich Opera House

different: here I was learning every day, and this was in great part
thanks to Alexander Pereira.

It does not surprise me that many people gave us no more than
three months. Even then, Pereira was known for his emotionalism
and his unconventional ego. Later, at the Salzburg Festival, my own
experiences with him were not all positive. But when one realises that
in all his actions he is driven by passion, that he always gets straight
to the point and in every situation he stands up lock, stock and barrel
for his house and his company, one learns to appreciate even his ego.

Alexander Pereira is an Austrian, like me. His parents wanted him
first to learn a 'proper' job, and so he became tourism manager and
then agent for the Italian typewriter company Olivetti. But his heart
belonged to music. Actually he would have liked to become a singer,
but in the end he made his career as a cultural manager. By way of
the Frankfurt Bach Concerts he came to the Vienna Konzerthaus.

Here he was successful, and made Christoph Lieben-Seutter, today director of the Elbphilharmonie in Hamburg, his assistant. From Vienna, Pereira moved on to the Zurich Opera House. His original career as an agent stood him in good stead as an opera director.

In the early 1980s the Zurich Opera House underwent a costly refurbishment and rebuilding programme. At the same time the city opposed the building of an autonomous youth centre. The result was the biggest and most radical youth protests in Swiss history. After a Bob Marley concert these culminated in the so-called Opera House riots, with numerous injuries on the part of both the young protesters and the police. When Pereira took over in Zurich, the dissent had subsided. He moved into a brand-new opera house and now sought his role in the international opera business.

What I particularly appreciate in Pereira is that not only is he an enthusiastic opera fan, who knows operatic literature, music and voices, but he is above all else a structural strategist. How often have I heard it said by patrons: 'I actually wanted to tell Alexander that I wanted to suspend my donations for a year, and when he left, I had signed an undertaking to pay even more than last year.' In Zurich he mobilised in particular the well-heeled major sponsors, banks, insurance companies and other large firms to fund his plans.

For Pereira, the structure of a house is the basis for artistic visions. And so, within the shortest possible time, he completely reorganised the management of the Zurich Opera House. Pereira played a significant part, by means of a popular vote, in transferring the house from the hands of the state into the hands of the canton, with its much greater financial liquidity. In this way he laid the foundations for a remarkable business model that still operates today. The Zurich Opera House is a limited company with more than 24,000 shareholders, none of whom owns more than 10 per cent of the 9,508 registered securities. The company runs the music theatre and ballet on behalf of the canton of Zurich.

Apart from this groundwork, Alexander Pereira fought to have the Zurich Opera House made a member of the German-speaking Opera Conference, now an association of 13 opera houses in Germany, Austria and Switzerland, whose artistic directors, business managers and other directors meet regularly to exchange experiences – a not insignificant network and a strong interest group.

My first contact with the Zurich Opera House was a repeat recording of Richard Strauss's *Rosenkavalier* in 1992. After this, the orchestra approached Alexander Pereira and asked for my appointment. He believed he could actually manage without a principal conductor. After Ferdinand Leitner and Ralf Weikert, it was the regularly appearing legendary conductors who had at first put their stamp on activities in Zurich – particularly Nello Santi, who had been at the Opera House since 1958 and concerned himself mainly with the Italian repertoire, and Nikolaus Harnoncourt, who appeared in Zurich from 1975, first with Monteverdi and later with Offenbach, Weber and even Verdi. I believe Pereira was sceptical when he offered me the post of principal conductor. At the same time, he was enough of a tactician to sense that he should respect the wish of the orchestra and could build on my curiosity. After all, I had hardly any experience with opera, but was more than eager to learn.

In the end, over a period of 13 years, with endless passion we continually developed new visions together and made Zurich into one of the leading opera houses in Europe. Working with Alexander Pereira was perhaps so successful because he was always concerned about the content. I remember many differences of opinion and quarrels, and sometimes things became heated. But we never argued over contracts, money or inner structures, only about line-ups, directors or singers. And in the end, with every decision we pulled together – both inside and outside the house.

Pereira loves excess, lavishness and a grand entrance. And so I would like to tell a story here which concerns a different kind of silence. It could be called 'When I silenced the Pope'. On 6 May 2006

Pope Benedict did not take offence over the faux pas at the Gloria when he received Franz Welser-Möst and his wife at a private audience after the performance of Mozart's Coronation Mass in May 2006

the solemn high mass was celebrated in St Peter's in Rome on the occasion of the 500th anniversary of the Swiss Guard in the Vatican. Thanks to his connections, above all the then president of Switzerland Moritz Leuenberger, Pereira had succeeded in obtaining agreement for the orchestra and choir of the Zurich Opera House to participate in this event. At the request of Pope Benedict XVI, Mozart's Coronation Mass and 'Laudate Dominum' were to be played. On that day, we had to be in the cathedral very early in the morning, for security checks, although the organisation of these seemed to be rather improvised and chaotic. We were placed behind the high altar in St Peter's, and the master of ceremonies at the Vatican informed me just before the ceremony began that the Holy Father would himself begin the singing of the Gloria. There followed the colourful entry of the Swiss

Guard, the cardinals, bishops, dignitaries and altar servers. At the end of this long procession the Pope appeared, diminutive almost to the point of invisibility.

In this overwhelming setting with its splendour and resounding echo, the liturgy of the Word began with all the pageantry that the Catholic Church offers for such occasions. In the first part of the Holy Mass I could not see the Pope, as we were on the other side of the gigantic high altar. We performed the Kyrie and then I waited for the Pope to begin the singing of the Gloria. I waited, it seemed for an eternity. I could not follow what was happening in front of the high altar, and when the cathedral organist intoned the Gloria, I thought, because of the chaos we had experienced in the run-up to the performance, that the master of ceremonies must have misinformed me, and I went ahead.

Afterwards Alexander Pereira told me, in consternation larded with reproaches, that at the precise moment when I began the jubilant Gloria, the Pope had just risen from his seat and already opened his mouth to begin singing the Gloria. So he simply sat down again. A real faux pas on my part, which I committed although I had grown up in the Catholic Church and had also been an altar boy for eight years. After the High Mass there was a private audience in the Pope's personal chambers, where President Leuenberger introduced me and my wife to Pope Benedict. When it was my turn and he held out his hand to me in greeting, I said: 'Holy Father, I'm sorry to have cut you short!' He smiled and replied: 'It was Mozart.'

It should be realised that the words 'small' and 'modest' do not appear in Alexander Pereira's vocabulary. And this can be seen in our respective records: he has sometimes included 16 premieres in a single season. For myself, I have taken over five premieres, and stood in the orchestra pit on 70 evenings, in one season. In my time in Zurich I conducted 43 premieres and 49 different productions – all this on far more than 500 evenings. This reveals much about the philosophy that he has followed and – it must be added – that the house could also afford financially. For us it was about multiplicity, a broad repertoire and as much variation as possible. Our calculations were straightforward: it was better for five out of 16 premieres to flop than for five out of six to fall flat with the public. At the same time, it was always Pereira's watchword to challenge the company. He liked to say: 'If the musicians and singers have no time to sit in the staff restaurant, they will not have a chance to conduct intrigues either.' Then he would give his broad smile with the gap between his middle teeth.

Alexander Pereira is a sort of Uli Hoeneß of opera [the long-time manager of the European star football club FC Bayern München], a strict boss with a big heart, a passionate and assertive manager, but also a soft-hearted supporter of his artists. I remember regular shouting matches with the ballet director Heinz Spoerli in the corridors of the Opera House; they were two alpha males who were constantly clashing. But I also recall some occasions when Pereira would telephone the *Neue Zürcher Zeitung* because some critic, no matter what we did, persisted in putting the orchestra and myself in a bad light. Pereira demanded a face-to-face discussion and fought like a lion for his people and his company – usually with great success. At the same time he had no inhibitions when it came to money. Once, two minutes before I was to appear at the entrance to the orchestra pit, he approached me and asked if I was happy with the fee for the DVD recording of this production. He knew that I was already fully focused on the performance and used this in a charming manner. Today I know that a large part of the international success of the Zurich Opera House was due to the fact that by means of DVD contracts Pereira made available to the world much of what happened there. Even if we did not earn excessive amounts, we all profited from this. Pereira himself described himself in my presence as someone who went around with his vendor's tray to offer his opera house to the whole world.

In the foreground of my time in Zurich was opera as *Gesamtkunstwerk*, the total work of art: a tight interplay between musical direction and experienced theatre directors such as Harry Kupfer, Robert Wilson, Götz Friedrich and Jürgen Flimm. At the same time, new ideas were nourished; for example, Sven-Eric Bechtolf directed his first opera for us with his spectacular production of Alban Berg's *Lulu*.

Always at the centre, however, were the singers. Inside the opera house, experience and youthful curiosity were intended to complement each other. This was one reason why the opera studio for young singers was of great importance, and why Alexander Pereira in particular did everything he could to ensure that the great legends of song felt at ease in Zurich (and that a large number of them even settled there). They could all rely on Pereira's unconditional loyalty.

There were legendary evenings at our Opera House, when the 70-year-old Hermann Prey yet again sang Papageno from *The Magic Flute*, or Alfredo Kraus at 71 took on Jules Massenet's *Werther*, sounding as though he was only 40 years old – a sensation for everyone who was present. I remember a performance of *Boris Godunov* in which Matti Salminen played the title role and Nicolai Ghiaurov the monk Pimen – an evening when the director David Pountney had no need to set the scene and I, as conductor, simply followed the two giants, open-mouthed. Ghiarov's wife, Mirella Freni, appeared alongside him in Zurich in Tchaikovsky's *Eugene Onegin*, and Pereira and I tried to fulfil even her most unusual requests. One of them was that she desperately wanted to sing *Madame Sans-Gêne* by Umberto Giordano, admittedly not a first-class opera. But because it was Freni (and there is always something to learn from her), Pereira put the piece on the programme – and as a result we were given a masterclass in matters of *Verismo*. The legendary singers were always able to pass on their experience to us, who were then able to absorb these lessons of discipline, honesty and authenticity.

When one looks at the lists of performers at that time, it is astonishing: Agnes Baltsa, Edita Gruberová, Cecilia Bartoli, Anja Silja,

Francisco Araiza, Thomas Hampson, Leo Nucci and Neil Shicoff were committed to the house – a mixture of veteran stars, artists at the height of their careers and young, ambitious singers who were eager to learn. I believe it is essential to put together such a stimulating mix at an ensemble house. Anyone accepted at the Zurich opera studio probably learned more on the big stage with the stars of singing than at any college of music. Pereira travelled the world and listened to an endless number of voices to find out what was happening at other opera houses, and to bring the most exciting voices back to Zurich. Here we then gave them the space they needed to develop freely. It was a time when a general music director would still discuss the repertoire together with the singers, when they would consider together which piece was ready to be performed and which opera they would rather postpone. Today, it seems to me, particularly in bigger houses, there seems to be no time for such deliberations. But it is exactly what builds a good opera house in the long term. It is a home, a family that can be trusted, a place where a voice can be nurtured rather than prematurely challenged and destroyed in the medium term. An opera house is ideally supported by many individuals, who in their different ways work together for a common purpose.

Particularly with the young company members we had – which we can admit to now – extremely good luck; whenever a *Magic Flute* was scheduled, we could choose between two tenors, the young Jonas Kaufmann and the young Piotr Beczala.

It was these areas of tension and the working atmosphere that made the Zurich Opera House such an extraordinary place. Everyone who worked there sensed that they were part of a special worldwide project. We had succeeded in creating a wonderful collaboration with each other, despite all the diversity and contrasts. And this is particularly due to the quality of the Zurich Opera Orchestra. It was important to me that the musicians benefited from the broad range of the house, that they would play on one evening with Nello Santi conducting, on the next with Nikolaus Harnoncourt, and on the third again with me. I had the luxury of providing my own variety: from Wagner's Ring in its entirety to operetta, from Mozart to Verismo. The selection of DVDs that came out during those years alone, shows the diversity of the house. Among our productions were Jonathan Miller's staging of *The Magic Flute*, *Simplicius* by Johann Strauss II, Schubert's *Fierabras* with Jonas Kaufmann and Juliane Banse, Debussy's *Pelléas et Mélisande*, Benjamin Britten's *Peter Grimes*, Verdi's *Macbeth* directed by David Pountney, Richard Wagner's *Mastersingers* with José van Dam and Peter Seiffert, Richard Strauss's *Arabella* with Renée Fleming, Eugen d'Albert's *Tiefland* directed by Matthias Hartmann, and, already mentioned, Sven-Eric Bechtolf's *Lulu*, which remains spectacular for me today, with Laura Aikin in the title role. I am sure that it was the orchestra's flexibility and diversity of sound which ensured that in 2002 it was chosen as opera orchestra of the year, which brought us increased international attention.

Ultimately, however, I sensed that it was becoming ever more difficult to make further demands on the by now saturated Zurich Opera House. Many procedures had become routine, and there was a danger of becoming complacent. My relationship with Alexander Pereira had also cooled off somewhat. In other words, it was time to take on a new challenge, and that meant saying goodbye. I did this with my last premiere of Richard Strauss's *Die Frau ohne Schatten*, and then finally with the conducting of the opera which had also been the first one I conducted at the Zurich Opera House, Richard Strauss's *Rosenkavalier*. When the curtain had fallen on this last performance, I said goodbye backstage to the wonderful orchestra, the superb ensemble, and the old warhorse Alexander Pereira, from whom I had learned so much, about how important both the structures and enduring enthusiasm are for the functioning of a first-class opera house. 'I thank Alexander Pereira,' I said in a little impromptu speech, 'the artistic director who is for me a mixture of the Sun King, Münchhausen, a carpet dealer and Mother Teresa.' A declaration of love for one of the strongest personalities I have known in the opera business.

Thoughts on director's theatre

Today we presumably read *The Magic Mountain* as Thomas Mann intended – word for word. And even the *Mona Lisa* smiles at us in the Louvre in Paris presumably as Leonardo intended – stroke by stroke. Nothing apart from the passage of time stands between these works of art and us, their recipients. In music, things are different – and particularly so in opera. Unlike a book or a painting, music must be recreated every evening. An opera has, if you like, two acts of creation. The first and most important takes place when the librettist commits the text, and the composer the notes, to paper. This first creation is the inevitable basis of the second creation, our work to bring the silent notes to life anew every evening through their musical and staged interpretation. The same opera, even if interpreted by the same company and the same conductor, will always sound different on two different evenings. Ultimately music is the art of the eternally different in what is always the same. Every evening the same notes – from Bach's *Brandenburg Concertos* to Schönberg's *Verklärte Nacht* – are played and they never sound the same. The question of how, as a conductor, one goes about dealing with this circumstance of a 'second creation' is one which I will examine more closely later. In the case of opera, this question is posed at least as radically for the scenic interpretation, that is, for the direction.

It is logical that we cannot perform an opera today in the same way as in the times of Mozart or Wagner. There are various reasons for this, above all that fact that our world has changed. Not only our values and dogmas have changed, but also our theatrical world and – not to be underestimated – its technology. Our theatres are larger, our singers are differently trained and we have completely new opportunities at our disposal. While Richard Wagner still had to rely on candlelight when Lohengrin made his entrance, today we have digitally operated spotlights. And there is no doubt that someone like Wagner, of all people, who coined the famous saying

'*Kinder, schafft Neues!*' (Children, make something new!), would have wholeheartedly embraced technological innovations. So the past is not an option for us. Even if we performed Mozart by candlelight, we ourselves would still be children of our time. Whether we wish it or not, we will never again be in a position to hear or feel as people did in Mozart's time. I have always liked Nikolaus Harnoncourt's explanation of this phenomenon: anyone who has heard the sound of an aircraft can no longer hear *Eine kleine Nachtmusik* as Mozart did. This is one reason why Harnoncourt's historically informed performance practice was never an attempt to imitate Mozart's time, but the eternal endeavour to make the essence of his music come alive in the present day. And that is a very different matter.

It is particularly for opera that this question is important. It can bridge the gap between the past and present: the score as a historically fixed point and its theatrical implementation as a present-day point of reference. Like a conductor, an orchestra or the singers, a director is always part of the 'second creation', that process through which alone a score can be experienced as an art in the present day. In a Salzburg Festival programme I found an article on directing opera by Lothar Wallerstein (1882-1949), a conductor and theatre and opera director from Prague who emigrated to the USA after the *Anschluss* of Austria. His spirited work as a director set new standards for the stage. From 1926 he also regularly staged productions at the Salzburg Festival, among them the *Rosenkavalier* and *Ariadne auf Naxos* in close collaboration with Hugo von Hofmannsthal and Richard Strauss. Referring to the director's 'mediating role' he said: 'The "stage directions", both printed and traditional, are often only a form of suggested representation, in addition still based on the time in which the work was created, and suited to the theatrical and technical opportunities of that time. Here the stylistically confident director should not be denied the right to make changes: all he is doing is to seek a new interpretation of the intellectual content of the work for *his* time, and thus act as mediator between the author and the present day.'

To forestall misunderstandings: the contemporaneity of an operatic production does not necessarily depend on whether the stage is peopled with aircraft, spaceships or extra-terrestrials, or whether the singers are wearing ripped jeans. There are thoroughly contemporary productions which are rooted in the past, just as there are very outdated ones in which the director has located the action on the moon. I find that the term 'director's theatre' basically causes confusion rather than defining a clear framework or a tangible aesthetic. It is obvious that every director wants to get through to the audience of his day – what language and means he uses in order to do this is, for me personally, of secondary importance and still says nothing about the quality of a production.

That we in the world of opera are still conducting a debate about director's theatre, in my opinion, is due to something other than the individual theatrical aesthetic. In reality, what we are discussing is a fundamental question of our time. At one time there was a consensus that theatres – and certainly city theatres – should be moral institutions, places where our view was directed at the world with the basic principles of humanism. It is this basic constellation that is increasingly tottering, in a world where there seems to be less and less agreement over moral conventions, or at least in which they are massively displaced.

In the discussion in this book on the education programme, I have already described my firm conviction that many people lack a system of coordinates in which to codify our ever more complex present day. A key question seems to me to be: how can we still orient ourselves collectively? What are the irrefutable moral categories in which we can all believe? Will there ever again be an aesthetic to which performances in our theatres can be directed? We live in a world in which, despite moving closer together in the wake of globalisation in many areas, we seem to be drifting apart. Fake news plays a role here. Even institutions such as the Catholic Church are called into question – both through knowledge of the behaviour of the 'ground crew', which does not obey its own rules, and a widespread scepticism about religion in itself. Populists and their movements are no longer minority phenomena, and the Church is losing its claim to be a majority moral institution. We are living in a time in which two doctrines are tottering simultaneously, which have marked our coexistence and at the same time our art and culture for centuries: humanism and religion.

Even what we used to call the 'European tradition' no longer exists in the same way. In the 1990s director's theatre, particularly in the USA, was equated with 'European trash'. At the time it was the so-called Movement of 1968, a German students' movement, which brought to the public eye an overdue political debate, which had been long avoided after the National Socialist period. As a result, in a further development we were for the first time able to experience Patrice Chéreau's gods as humans in the centenary production of the *Ring* at Bayreuth in 1976. Today it is difficult to imagine that this director's concept was greeted as a scandal with whistling and booing, and accompanied by pandemonium.

Presumably we have found the freedom we were seeking. But what we have forgotten is that freedom is a sister of the sense of responsibility – responsibility for oneself, but also for others. Under the slogan of provocation, which was so decisive for decades in the so-called German director's theatre, we have forgotten that with these provocations we have only created new images of an enemy. Opposition excludes cooperation and thus contradicts the original idea of the theatre.

How can we fight the general erosion of the theatre? After the Movement of 1968 we tried postmodernism, eclecticism, that is, the frantic citation of the past and the established. This may perhaps have been an entertaining temporary fashion, but today we know that it often self-referentially went round in circles. I am of the strong opinion that a world which is caught up in radical change could make good use of the theatre in three ways: consciousness of the significance and functioning of our institutions, perfect craftsmanship and a coherent narration. These are three essential building blocks which would be good not only for the operatic stage, but also for politics.

The most unerring criterion here is the craftsmanship. The whole company in a piano dress rehearsal should not have to deal with the question of how the dead Commendatore in *Don Giovanni* actually gets off the stage. This is a question that the director should already have solved before the first rehearsal! It is no secret that during my time at the Vienna State Opera I had problems with the Mozart productions of the director Jean-Louis Martinoty, and after his *Figaro* and *Don Giovanni* I declined to direct *Così* as well. But here I am not talking about an individual case but about the basics of the director's work: when opera functions well, it is one of the most beautiful of all forms of art, but when it does not, it can be one of the most dreadful. There are so many cogs in the wheel that have to connect seamlessly each evening, and for all this there must be a framework, a content-related connection between the various levels of this complex *Gesamtkunstwerk* with regard to music, text, movement and image. I believe that in this way opera can certainly handle disagreements and differences of opinion, but that the process of making an opera should always be a combined effort. And here it is important that every part of this great machine should feel responsible, should be included in the process of creation, and also, of its own accord, should demand information and an exchange of views. If this basic precondition is not present, I personally am not keen to take my place at the conductor's stand.

I remember a set design rehearsal of Richard Strauss's opera *Arabella* in Zurich, at which I, as conductor of the opera, was present. This surprised the director, Götz Friedrich. 'What are you doing here?' he asked. When I replied that this rehearsal was my last chance to exert my influence on the stage and see if it corresponded to my acoustic expectations, he replied: 'Of course you are right, but I have never seen a conductor at a set design rehearsal before.'

For me this has always been something obvious, like my wish to exchange views with the director about the musical and stage interpretation, even before the first rehearsals. I also expect from directors knowledge of, or at least an interest in, the music. What is difficult for me to understand is when a Don Ottavio asks the director: 'What shall we do in this scene, there is so much music to get through?' and the director answers: 'Just try something out.' I do not think it is the singers' job to explain the opera to the director. So for me it is totally reasonable that singers – who are expected to appear fully prepared on the first day of rehearsal – should refuse to rehearse on stage for six to eight weeks when the director has not done any preparation. Quite generally, the complexity of opera is often underestimated, above all by directors who have not worked within this genre before. I feel sceptical when directors do not prepare themselves with the score but only with a CD booklet.

I am firmly convinced that, precisely at a time which is growing louder and more chaotic, awareness of the epic and the return of craftsmanship must gain in significance – and in particular our individual attitude.

It is important for me that art should never become hermetic. It cannot be a question of imposing a single idea of a director on a work. Art is exciting for me only when it remains open – even in its complexity. Interpretation means taking the observer by the hand and leading them into the sphere of fantasy. All art should allow space for the audience to think for themselves and not impose a finished image on them. I remember the reactions to Sven-Eric Bechtolf's production of *Lulu* in Zurich. At the point in the opera where a film is shown, Bechtolf showed a video in which a girl is running away from a man's hand which is reaching for her. After the premiere we received a number of letters from audience members, including one in which someone complained that we had shown 'the rape of a child'. For me this was a surprising reaction, showing that the individual imagination can extend far beyond what is actually observed – for no act of rape was ever to be seen on our screen.

I appreciate productions that are timeless. 'Timeless' means for me that the element of freedom from time, which is intrinsic to every great work of art, can be experienced in a production, together with a convincing and consistent concept of space. Here I like to think, among many others, of *Fidelio* or *Tannhäuser*, on which I worked with Claus Guth, the *Rosenkavalier* at Salzburg with Harry Kupfer or *Salome* with Romeo Castellucci.

Since we are now discussing the institution of opera in itself, it is perhaps important to remember that the opera houses have certainly themselves created some of the problems which they currently face. Conditions for rehearsals deteriorated drastically when the opera houses began to slash payments to artists for rehearsals. This resulted in a cycle which has adversely affected the quality of many productions up to now. Since artists are no longer paid for rehearsal time, but per performance, they try to minimise the number of rehearsals they are prepared to attend. And so there is less and less rehearsal. For economic reasons, the theatres are increasing the number of performances within a shorter amount of time But here too, it should be considered that it is precisely in a shrill, pressured world that art is perhaps the last place which should allow itself the luxury of rest and relaxation. Where else?

The Da Ponte cycle in Salzburg in 2013 was a labour of love, for which I had really battled in advance. But suddenly, when it came to it, I was in a position of musical responsibility and could not allow three performances to be given within less than five days. I had learned from the past that timings like these simply do not allow the relaxation necessary for the artists and the art. For this reason, too, I had to cancel my cooperation with Alexander Pereira, who had in the meantime become musical director of the Salzburg Festival. The opera productions of the last years in Salzburg had become for me

Rehearsals for the new production of *Lear* by Aribert Reimann (left)
at the Salzburg Festival in 2017

increasingly a confirmation that opera can best fulfil its function
under work conditions which, as with *Fidelio*, Aribert Reimann's
Lear, the *Rosenkavalier* and *Salome*, filled me with great pleasure and
were artistically very satisfying.

When we think of the theatrical stage as the stage of the world, and
believe that opera is not just the wallpaper of a modern entertainment
society, but should continue to foster the ambition to order our lives,
our longings and our sufferings so that they provide an orientation
for our present day, then this art needs exactly what our age lacks:
great restfulness and the endless ability to breathe.

Wiener "Wahn" (from Richard Wagner)

In the history of the Vienna State Opera there is a whole series of directors and music directors who have offered their resignation. And at 10.15 on 5 September 2014 I too was standing in the office of Dominique Meyer, the director of the State Opera. A cosily furnished room with a big wall filled with books, an oil painting of Gustav Mahler and a view of the Opernplatz. The evening before, there had been a final attempt, on the initiative of the then chief executive of the Bundestheater-Holding, Günter Rhomberg, to find a workable plan for further collaboration between Meyer and myself, by means of a conversation between the three of us. But the rifts were too deep. It is always difficult to draw a line under something, but ultimately I had no alternative. So next morning I knocked on Dominique Meyer's door and handed him a envelope. 'What's this?' he asked me, and I replied: 'My resignation.' At that moment he smiled, and as I added: 'I have become convinced that you never wanted to have a general music director,' he commented: 'That's not the case.' Dominique Meyer placed the envelope on his round desk, and I left his office without a further word.

After that, everything went very fast. In a statement to the Austrian press agency I explained my resignation from this post: 'There are differences about the artistic direction of the house which have not arisen overnight. Dominique Meyer is a first-class director. He is a very nice person who just has different opinions in artistic matters. That is his right. But I have to take the consequences.' Dominique Meyer's announcement stated that he had received my resignation 'with great regret', a step about which he was 'very sorry', since he 'valued Franz Welser-Möst very highly as an artist and conductor'.

It seemed as though, in the days that followed, for some persons in authority in the house my departure could not come quickly enough. I was in the middle of a tour with the Cleveland Orchestra and was requested to clear out my office immediately and to hand in my key and the chip for the doors of the State Opera.

From one moment to the next, Dominique Meyer was faced with the huge challenge of appointing other conductors for 34 evenings and two premieres. I have often been asked why I left so abruptly. It had not escaped me that there was an increasing split in the house, and I was convinced that this rift should not be further deepened by my presence.

Seven years earlier, in 2007 – I was in Cleveland at the time – I had been somewhat surprised to receive the offer from Claudia Schmied, the then minister of culture, of the post of general music director at this unique opera house. I remember the telephone call from Vienna, which roused great emotions in me: to be able to work in this house, so rich in tradition, which is furnished with such incredible artistic potential, and positively invites creativity like no other – and for me as an Austrian! I asked for some time to think, since I knew Dominique Meyer only by name and from what I had heard about him. My first telephone conversation with him, in my judgement, was conducted in a very promising manner. So I accepted, and thought that here, at the very top level of the opera world, was where I could bring in my ideas and visions based on the wonderful experiences I had had in Zurich.

Dominique Meyer was charged by the Ministry to negotiate the contract with me. In a protracted process over several months we tried to define our respective roles as clearly as possible, to avoid any friction and ambiguity in the future. I have always been of the opinion, even when contracts are known to be lenient, that all problems that arise in a partnership can be talked through. 'The general music director', it says in my contract, 'will be included in good time in the decision processes relevant to him, and will receive in good time the information he needs.' We also added a passage with the explicit instruction that decisions about singers, artistic staff, repertoire and directors should be made in agreement between the artistic director and the general music director.

It is probably impossible to exclude later differences of opinion in the contract in advance. With Alexander Pereira I had never looked anything up in my contract. We were not always of the same opinion, but we found solutions and continued to plough ahead together.

In 2007, when we were appointed, the sun was still shining. At the press conference, Dominique Meyer said that it was too soon after our appointment to present any concrete plans, as this was still the time for dreams for us. I had many of these: I wanted to implant Leoš Janáček and other important 20th-century operas in the repertoire, I wanted to have all the operas of Richard Strauss performed in a single season, and place dramatic emphases which would correspond to the great tradition of the house, I wanted to see exceptional colleagues at the conductor's stand… In Zurich I had seen how important it was to support ideas with structures and develop a common strategy. In Vienna, too, I wanted the artistic line of approach to be laid down for the coming years. But as soon as the second year of preparation dawned it became clear that there were differences of opinion over questions of planning, not least of which was the engagement of first-class artists. So I wrote to Meyer: 'I understand if you say you do not want to propose a five-year plan, but I believe that certain basic features should be defined and reasonable. Otherwise the Vienna Opera will have to be content with too many second- and third-rate artists.' Gradually it turned out that we had different approaches to basic strategies of running an opera house, and also the issue of the direction of this unique house and how it should position itself internationally.

Even the first season was marked by far too many compromises on my part. I got my own way with Paul Hindemith's *Cardillac* as the first premiere of our first season, which was a great success despite all the prophecies of doom. But Meyer persuaded me to take over *Don Giovanni* and then *The Marriage of Figaro*, which Riccardo Muti had originally been going to conduct. While he loved these two productions, they nearly drove me to despair. That it was over Mozart, the 'god of opera', who was so important to Vienna, of all composers, that the first clouds were gathering, still saddens me today. Our aesthetic, artistic and conceptual standards diverged to a substantial degree. One thing led to another, and despite all our attempts to find a common artistic and aesthetic path, we increasingly drifted apart.

One is always wiser in retrospect, and from today's viewpoint I should have noticed many things earlier and drawn the consequences. At first there were trivialities, such as when I discovered the negotiations over the hiring of singers were concluded when I was not in Vienna. In general, Meyer's method of selecting the singers did not please me. He was present at many auditions, even when it was obvious that the singers in question would not fulfil the necessary quality criteria. So I asked him to audition only those who had been found suitable in a preliminary screening by the appropriate artistic team. If simply for reasons of efficiency, we should listen just to these ones together. I believe that for Meyer these auditions were a kind of recreation after all the administrative work that is mandatory for a director of a house of this stature.

At first I still tried to address the problems, but this became more difficult each time. Unfortunately many of my questions, both spoken and in writing, remained unanswered. It was a gruelling process, which ultimately led to my resignation, since my dreams, ideas, aims and visions had been crushed.

Nevertheless, my work with what was probably the best operatic orchestra in the world, the wonderful State Opera choir and also many singers in the company whom I was able to accompany, in some cases for years, was extremely rewarding – a cooperation that I have missed since resigning. It was a great pleasure for me not only to discover singers, but also to support them in their development over the years with my advice. In 2006 the legendary Ioan Holender, known for his strong personality and unconventional opinions, said with reference to the search for a singer for the role of Alberich in Wagner's *Ring*: 'If there is no singer for a role, one has to be invented!' At that time, we 'invented' Tomasz Konieczny.

From the early 2000s I had increasing contact with Ioan Holender. It was he who invited me in September 2003 to stand in overnight, without a rehearsal, for Christian Thielemann in *Tristan and Isolde*, and there followed the premieres of *Arabella*, the entire *Ring*, and *Tannhäuser* in his era as State Opera director. I learned a great deal from him, above all that one must have imagination, courage and the ability to recognise potential.

Another reason why the Vienna State Opera is so exceptional is the high degree of artistic consciousness in the house. For me, not only was playing with the State Opera orchestra a great pleasure, but so also was the readiness of the orchestra to negotiate the rehearsal schedule with its trade union. One needs to bear in mind that the activity in a house of this kind, with around 300 performances during the ten months when it is open, and some 50 different operas on each season's schedule, is extremely complex. In order to organise the 148 musicians and their necessary assistants, each instrument group in the orchestra needs a person responsible for producing the staff roster and assigning their colleagues to their roles. We met – and this was a major innovation in this business – once in every season to discuss the next one. The aim was to assign roles for the rehearsals and performances from artistic and not only organisational viewpoints, thus introducing more efficiency into the repertoire system. In each season, new and rarely performed works, which require intensive rehearsal work with as little change as possible in the orchestra line-up, alternate on the schedule with works which are part of the great canon of the opera repertoire, such as *The Magic Flute*, the *Rosenkavalier* or *Traviata*, and thus, as standard repertoire, require fewer rehearsals, without loss of quality in the performances. I have always been a great champion of the Vienna State Opera's repertoire system, since, among other things, it preserves the flexibility and autonomy of each musician, and thus the invariable personality of this collective.

Another example of the high degree of artistic consciousness and conscientiousness of this orchestra was the penultimate rehearsal for the premiere of Janáček's *Káťa Kabanová* at the end of my first season. The rehearsal went badly, which was partly due to the fact that some musicians had not had enough rehearsal time and were not sufficiently familiar with this very difficult work. We played the piece through once, which took just over 90 minutes, and took a break. I sent the singers home and rehearsed with only the orchestra for another two and a half hours without a further break. This was contrary to the provisions of the collective agreement, but everyone, absolutely everyone, cooperated without saying a word. On top of that, after this very demanding rehearsal the union shop steward came to me and asked me, after the last public rehearsal with the orchestra, to continue working and polishing our performance, which we did.

I believe that the high standards of these musicians derive from their dual function as members of the orchestra of the Vienna State Opera and of the Vienna Philharmonic. The Vienna Philharmonic is organised as a private society, which is democratically run and self-governing. This entails artistic autonomy, a long tradition which affects the mentality and mindset of the individual musicians and their self-confidence. This particular characteristic is also connected with the fact that outside the opera, that is, as the private society of the Vienna Philharmonic, they never had a principal conductor. Since 1933 there was never only one conductor who determined the artistic activity of the orchestra. I was able to experience their intensive collaboration with Karl Böhm, Herbert von Karajan and Leonard Bernstein in the eras of the 1960s, 1970s and 1980s. They took from each conductor what seemed valuable to them, but were at the same time capable of giving to each of these different maestros what they demanded. The symbiosis of Vienna State Opera Orchestra/ Vienna Philharmonic is seen in the special quality of the musicians in the orchestra pit of this house with its rich tradition, and with its responsiveness to the particular vocal articulation of the singers – I am firmly convinced – makes a huge contribution to the soft, lyrical,

Rehearsals for the premiere of Janáček's *Káťa Kabanová* in Franz Welser-Möst's
first season (2010/11) at the Vienna State Opera

golden sound of the Vienna Philharmonic and its special flexibility,
spontaneity and quick reactions.

Thanks to this orchestra, the performances in the pit of the Vienna
State Opera could become small musical miracles, sometimes even
moments of glory. I remember some of these, especially on evenings
when everything seemed be working against such moments. Just one
example: on the evening after the New Year's Day concert of 2013,
Ariadne auf Naxos was to be performed with the wonderful Krassimira
Stoyanova. The orchestra and I myself were thoroughly exhausted

after the exertions of the previous days. During the first part of the performance this was noticeable. But after the interval, one of those 'Viennese miracles' happened which cannot be explained. It was as if we were different people, and the performance 'took off', as we call it. Something I will never forget!

I saw that this symbiosis was in danger before I took up my post. I learned that the Vienna State Opera orchestra was earning 30 per cent less by international comparison than, for example, the orchestra of the Bavarian State Opera in Munich. And this put it in danger of losing its competitive position and having to accept the departure of young musicians. The minister, Claudia Schmied, had promised me before Christmas in 2009 that this situation would be rectified with the help of a substantial increase in salaries. After all it was not a question of what these musicians were able to earn in addition in their free time as members of the Vienna Philharmonic, but that the remuneration to the State Opera was well below comparable international conditions.

When I returned to Vienna in March 2010, just before the first press conference of the designated new state opera direction, nothing had yet happened. I informed all participants that if a solution was not found, I would announce my resignation at this press conference. There were intense negotiations, and shortly before midnight the evening before the conference, the then chairman of the Vienna Philharmonic, Clemens Hellsberg, rang me, happy to report that an agreement had been reached.

My relationship with the Vienna Philharmonic was not love at first sight. My debut at the Salzburg Mozartwoche in 1999 with, among other works, Mozart's Piano Concerto K. 203, with Murray Perahia, and his Symphony No. 34 K. 338, had been far from a success. Nevertheless they invited me again, and many of the musicians see my standing in with *Tristan and Isolde* in 2003 as the moment when the ice was broken between us. Despite the many opera evenings, concerts, tours, as well as the two New Year's Day concerts to which they invited me – a few more words on this later – for me it was with the *Rosenkavalier* in Salzburg, in the summer of 2014, that I felt very close to this wonderful orchestra. I had made it with them as a musician.

In other respects this was a very intensive year. In March my mother died. In early summer, I signed a renewal of my contract for a further five years in Cleveland; in the same summer I was in Salzburg conducting my mother's favourite opera, the *Rosenkavalier*. My resignation followed in September, and my father died in November.

During this summer of 2014, musically so fulfilling, the dark clouds over the Vienna State Opera gathered ever more ominously. The feeling that my relationship with Dominique Meyer was becoming increasingly fraught did not deceive me. Up to the last, I tried to bring about a meeting to clear the air. Every year since our appointment in 2007 I had invited him to visit us at the Attersee, but he never followed up, although every summer he spent several days in nearby Salzburg. So it was in Salzburg that we met on 15 August for what turned out to be a penultimate attempt to change course. We were very polite and pleasant to each other, but more and more distant from each other on the subject under discussion.

However much I had wanted to move things on at the Vienna Opera, however often in the preceding months I had held conversations with persons of authority in the cultural sphere, on the night before 5 September I was finally forced to realise that I could no longer allow myself to be diverted from my artistic convictions. Resignation seemed to be the only way of finding my true self again.

Orchestras as mirrors of the world

I gave a great deal of thought to the concept of orchestra before I took over the Cleveland Orchestra in 2002. There is hardly another collective that can be as differently organised and structured as an orchestra. In the USA I became familiar with what was for me an entirely new model: an orchestra that lives for the most part on the support of enthusiastic citizens and businesses, and is run by the so-called board, which consists exclusively of private individuals.

After 11 September 2001, the attacks on the Twin Towers in New York, the USA sustained psychological damage, and the economy reacted nervously too. In Cleveland the economic blood-letting could be sensed; large firms moved away. When the great financial crisis of 2008/9 shook the world like an earthquake, our institution had to record a huge shortfall in its budget. Twenty per cent of our income had vanished. When Gary Hanson, the artistic director at the time, described the seriousness of the situation to me – it felt life-threatening – I had to set an example, and waived 20 per cent of my income until the institution could recover financial stability. In artistic respects, too, we had to change our plans and make savings, but covertly. Expensive programmes were replaced by others that were more economic, and those that we thought would be difficult to sell by more popular choices. Furthermore, vacancies in the management and one free position in the orchestra were not filled. We had to tighten our belts for one or two years and demonstrate entrepreneurial responsibility. It is humbling to observe how a crisis brings everyone closer together, in order to ensure corporate survival. The crises in 2001 and 2008/9 have taught me that at such times the in-house priority list, artistic convictions and the self-concept of the institution are put to the test. If I look at Cleveland, I am in an optimistic mood. A city with such a close relationship with its wonderful orchestra knows what the orchestra means to it. The confidence that we are there for each other is paramount.

Every orchestra functions differently, and is a very individual formation. There are self-governing and highly structured ensembles, bodies of musicians that are financed by the state or by radio licence fees, opera orchestras and youth orchestras. Each orchestra has different standards, rituals, working schedules and sensitivities.

I gained my first experience as a conductor with the Jeunesse Orchestra in Linz, an ensemble that consisted mainly of young

Rehearsals at St Florian Abbey with the Cleveland Youth Orchestra as part of their European tour in the summer of 2019

musicians. We took great pleasure in making music together and working on a challenging repertoire, such as Anton Bruckner's 5th Symphony. Most of us were students or had just completed our studies, had not yet started a family and treated music as a serious hobby. Working hours did not present a problem at the time. We often rehearsed for up to 12 hours a day, and even after such a long day we often continued to sit together and exchange thoughts about what we had worked on and experienced.

With my subsequent positions at the Winterthur City Orchestra and in Lausanne, things were different, as they were at Norrköping in Sweden. Here the orchestra had had no principal conductor for 13 years, but did have a strong trade union. For me this was totally new territory. Suddenly I had to keep to rehearsal times prescribed by collective agreements. But by means of private agreements with the union I could work for 12 hours with the musicians on the first day of every week of rehearsals, by dividing up the rehearsals into three-hour units, for high and low strings, woodwinds and brass. I learned that it makes sense for an orchestra to protect itself from work that gets out of hand, but have also noticed that one's own passion can open many doors. Some of the most beautiful work we achieved together in Norrköping was the rehearsal time for two concert performances of Richard Wagner's *Tristan and Isolde*. We had six weeks of rehearsals, and in the end all the musicians knew what was needed for their own parts as well as for the whole score. Just recently, by chance I heard a recording of this production, and was pleasantly surprised by the confident vitality of the evening and the technical standard of the performance.

I have already given an account of my time in London. What I learned there about orchestra structures was a totally different concept. In contrast to Austria or Germany, the orchestral landscape in Britain is based not on a philharmonic tradition, but on a more individualistic and privately operated music culture. The conductor Sir Thomas Beecham alone founded the New Symphony Orchestra, the London Philharmonic and the Royal Philharmonic Orchestras, three bodies of musicians, two of which still inform the national orchestral culture. Much of this reminds me of the capitalist superlative of the Baroque era of a George Frideric Handel, when it was a question of engaging as spectacular artists with as spectacular fees as possible, in order to satisfy the sensation-loving public. One might say that the system of the Baroque opera champions league was a version of the mercenarism that we still know today in sport, particularly in football: millionaires can afford to buy a club, and try to engage the best and most expensive players in the world for huge sums. In these conditions, an orchestra operates less as a company that draws on its traditional roots (such as the Vienna or Berlin Philharmonic), but remains a snapshot in time, constantly reinventing itself, whose potential must be related to that of the market. There are similar structures outside England too, for example in Switzerland, where the wealthy legal scholar and passionate amateur conductor Edmond de Stoutz founded the Zurich Chamber Orchestra largely for the purpose of his personal fulfilment.

One of the finest orchestral models for me, apart from the traditional Philharmonic orchestras, is the radio orchestra. It illustrates the naturalness of a body of musicians in the social structure. This tradition began in the 1920s in Germany as a side effect of the development of broadcasting – it was that period which saw the foundation of the Radio Symphony Orchestra Leipzig (now MDR Leipzig Radio Symphony Orchestra), the Berlin Radio Orchestra (now Berlin Radio Symphony Orchestra), and the Frankfurt Radio Symphony Orchestra (now HR Sinfonieorchester or Frankfurt Radio Symphony).

The initial idea was that of basic provision of music to all citizens, that is, what I am calling naturalness or a matter of course in everyday life. These orchestras were also founded in order to accommodate as many works as possible, so that the radio stations could have a programme at all. The radio orchestras brought music into the living room and were media in the truest sense of the word. They provided an opportunity to create community through music. Every living room could become a concert hall.

Today these orchestras are still financed by the television licences paid for by the public, and are thus part of the state cultural programme. This means that it is not only works by Beethoven and Brahms that are played. And so it is not by chance that the radio orchestras are open to new repertoires. They have promoted forms such as the radio opera, play at new music festivals, and foster composers such as Bohuslav Martinů and Hans Werner Henze, as does the Vienna Radio Symphony Orchestra (the orchestra of ORF, the Austrian national broadcaster Österreichischer Rundfunk), for example, and thus reach an audience entirely of their own.

It is all the more tragic to see that these orchestras at present are being challenged, closed down or merged with others. In Germany alone, this trend has affected, among others, the RIAS Symphony Orchestra, the symphony orchestras of the Süddeutscher Rundfunk and Südwestfunk radio stations, the Leipzig Radio Symphony Orchestra and the orchestra of the Hessischer Rundfunk station in Frankfurt. This is to say nothing of other countries in which the state cultural programme is under even greater scrutiny: in Italy, under the government of Silvio Berlusconi, some 20 per cent of cultural institutions were closed down, and of the four orchestras of the RAI (Radiotelevisione italiana) broadcasting company, only one remained.

The example of the radio orchestra teaches us that the existence of a collectively financed body of musicians has for a long time no longer been a matter of course in our society. This on the one hand is due to the new role of the media, particularly the alternatives of internet and streaming services. But one must also ask why the broadcasters have so little idea of how to position their radio orchestras in public – after all, there is no lack of broadcasting opportunities. Is it not astonishing that transmission and streaming of concerts by radio orchestras, which once quite as a matter of course formed the output of music broadcasting, today tend to be the exception? That radio orchestras hardly play a role any more in regional television stations? I do not understand why the institutions which can afford expensive ensembles do not present them via the media – and do not, as originally envisaged, provide them as a major part of their own programme. Fundamentally the idea of the basic provision of music is after all very sensible and praiseworthy. It would, I am certain, decidedly have a role, and particularly so in these digital times.

There is little point in insisting on traditional roles and rights. Rather, orchestras must face the regular question as to their relevance. And here we come full circle with the orchestra in Cleveland and a country such as the USA. Here it is a matter of course for a music director to give thought to the meaningfulness of his company,

Great artistic and creative effort is required to fill the magnificent
Severance Hall in Cleveland for a whole season

to understand his task not as 'God-given' (or state-given), but to
realise that he must repeatedly justify it to society. This can be a very
demanding process, in which one makes things easy for oneself by
considering the satisfaction of the mainstream, but it can also be a
very enlightening one when it is a question of arousing enthusiasm
in people for one's own, perhaps more ambitious path.

When I was invited to take over the Cleveland Orchestra, it was
important for me to ask myself these questions in advance. With this

in mind, I first addressed the history of the orchestra. I particularly liked the story of the foundation of Severance Hall. In December 1928 the oil magnate John Long Severance and his wife Elisabeth donated a million dollars for a new concert hall. When Elisabeth suddenly and unexpectedly died a month later, this hall became a sort of Taj Mahal of music. The interior decoration of the hall was based on Elisabeth Severance's wedding dress. The first music played at a rehearsal on 4 February 1930 in this acoustically and visually unique hall was the Prelude and *Liebestod* from Richard Wagner's *Tristan and Isolde*. These pieces were played at the request of John Long Severance in memory of his wife. This story moves me deeply every time I tell it.

The concert hall has a seating capacity of 2,000, and requires great creative effort on the part of our team in charge of artistic planning, marketing and PR to fill these seats for a whole season, while maintaining high standards in the construction of a programme.

My reflections on naturalness and the role of the orchestra were assisted by another look at history. The Cleveland Orchestra was founded in 1918 by Adella Prentiss Hughes with the aim of enriching the city through musical education. Sometimes it is so simple and logical to start with one's own roots in order to develop visions for the future. I have already written about the education work in Cleveland, and also about the fact that the development of quality in the orchestra is at least as important a concern.

A lovely story has circulated in Cleveland about Nikolai Sokoloff, the orchestra's first music director. Sokoloff was born in Kiev, studied at Yale, ran the San Francisco People's Philharmonic Orchestra, and had been leader of the Russian Symphony Orchestra, which was based in New York. His rule of three as a conductor in Cleveland was fairly simple: 'Be on time. Love your work. And watch me.' As far as the sound of the orchestra is concerned, however, the fourth general music director in Cleveland, George Szell, was probably especially influential. He took over the orchestra in 1946 and ran it until his death in 1970. It is thanks in large part to conductors such as Szell and his colleague Fritz Reiner in Chicago, Eugene Ormandy and his predecessor Leopold Stokowski in Philadelphia, that the American ideal of sound today stands for precision in teamwork. As early as 1912 Stokowski was music director in Philadelphia, and became a legend through his later work with Walt Disney in the animated film *Fantasia*. The American sound derives mainly from conductors who had their beginnings in Europe, but then had to emigrate for political reasons and came to the USA. The perfection to which American orchestras aspire also seems to me a sort of compensation for the lost European tradition. It is certain that Szell, who defined the combination of American precision and European musical tradition as his highest aim, after 24 years of leading the Cleveland Orchestra must have been a sort of father figure for his successors. I too was aware of his great heritage when I decided to go to the USA. But 32 years after Szell's death it was also clear that it must be possible to think in a new way. I remember a very pointed remark by the artistic director of the time, Tom Morris, which finally convinced me. He said: 'In Cleveland you have a big opportunity not to be a successor to George Szell.' What Morris meant was that the orchestra too had become ready for new visions and wanted to free itself from the shadow of the past. That pleased me. I hope that my successor will seek his own path and not only guard my heritage. After all, music is always the expression of the moment and of a time. It must continue to be written from generation to generation.

This continuation meant for me the preservation of the technical brilliance, precision and transparency found in and practised by my predecessors. But I also saw the need for cultural change: away from the authoritarian methods of the 1960s, and towards a greater individual sense of responsibility on the part of the individual musician and greater mutual respect – towards each other as well as towards their boss. According to an old joke about George Szell among musicians in Cleveland, even the pillars stood at attention when he entered the hall. I wanted to replace this sort of culture with a more human one – for one thing, from the conviction that we could not be relevant to society in the 21st century if we made use of the manners of a bygone age in our own house. Instead of an army of uniformed underlings, I wanted a collective of sensitive, musically intelligent individualists, who listened to each other and could immerse themselves in a work in the spirit of the highest principle that lies at the basis of all music-making: give and take.

A cultural change of this kind is a slow process, similar to the work of a gardener who must allow time and care for the plants to grow. My aim, apart from preserving all the splendid qualities that I found, was that the musicians should react more flexibly when playing and act more independently, thus achieving a warmer and more colourful sound. This is something one can attain with a purposefully introduced repertoire. The classical repertoire, for example works by Haydn, Mozart and Schubert, lends itself well to clarity and cleanness of interaction. For flexibility, the operatic genre is of particular value. It also encourages warmth of sound and the breath associated with it. In my first season, for example, we were already playing *Don Carlo*. Since then, opera has been an annual fixed point of the programme. The French repertoire offers outstanding opportunities for a wealth of tonal colours, since the blending of colours in sound is an essential, often dominating element of this music.

The greatest praise that I have received in the last 18 years in Cleveland came from our orchestra leader, who once said: 'Franz, no one writes any more that we have a "cold sound". Instead everyone writes about the "beauty of the strings". And indeed I agree that during these years the Cleveland Orchestra, while retaining its character, has newly defined its sound.

The characteristics of an orchestra and the change in its sound are also fascinating because each orchestra is an acoustic reflection of its time and its home. Our age is characterised by globalisation. Journeys are shorter, international exchange is universal – the world is shrinking. All of this has an influence on the culture of sound, in particular on somewhat less prominent or traditional orchestras. We are used to the sound of an orchestra being marked by regional or national influences. The Russian–Jewish violin school is such a phenomenon – its influence on the European sound is immense. I consider it a splendid opportunity of our time that the paths of the world have become shorter and faster to travel, and I do not believe that this must change the specific sounds of an orchestra. In the end, it is the musicians and conductor who autonomously decide the sound. For me, the opportunities for exchange are a big opportunity, which admittedly requires the precise knowledge of the language we want to speak with our orchestras.

For ultimately, traditional ideals of sound are nothing other than musical languages and dialects which can be learned. It is wrong to state that a musician from Tokyo cannot play like one in Munich. The horn section in Cleveland sounds quite different from the one in Chicago, although instruments from the same manufacturers are played in both cities. And it does no harm to the typical Viennese sound of the Vienna Philharmonic if the leader of the orchestra is from Leipzig. Admittedly, the question of regional or national sound cultures and their maintenance is no longer a given. In a globalised world, the possibilities increase, and this means that we have individual choice and the responsibility for making a decision ourselves as to how an orchestra should sound.

The last 18 years in Cleveland have been intensive with the orchestra as an institution – a time which has moulded, not only the ensemble, but also the conductor. I have learned much in the USA, above all that it is important repeatedly to address the relevance and self-concept of an institution such as an orchestra. Today the Cleveland Orchestra, despite crises, is in good shape and enjoys great approval, both in the city and also in Ohio, in the USA and at our guest appearances throughout the world. Orchestras are reflections of our time and must react to our times – they store experiences

Orchestras as reflections of their time: the Cleveland Orchestra's
100th season in 2017 opened with the opera *The Cunning Little Vixen*
with an animated stage set

(of sound) and have to define themselves anew every evening. In Cleveland I have learned that conductors are well advised if they are not concerned about conducting alone, but about the role of an orchestra in society. What we have to offer to society is to reflect on our existence through the emotions that music creates in us, and perhaps also to discover an inner compass in the process.

Second journey

The nature of silence

One of the most beautiful moments for me, outside music, is the start of a new day. I am an early riser, and often wake before 5am, put on walking shoes and warm clothes, and leave the house. Then I wander through the remains of the darkness, through the silence. A silence which is different from that in music, different from that of yoga, for in the early morning I am in fact already walking through a diverse backdrop of noises: the wind rustling in the trees, the animals that scurry through the woods at the first sign of dawn, my shoes, under whose soles the twigs break, or which jostle a stone aside. The sounds of nature increase abruptly when the red streaks of sunrise appear in the sky, when black is ousted by colour and the moon by the rising sun. When the birds awake and the heavens display their infiniteness – when a new day comes into being. This too is music for me.

I am not a tree-hugger, nor do I follow some esoteric cult of nature, but I consciously seek out this moment of the emerging day. For it is here that I repeatedly experience a dialogue with nature and my own being. Nowhere does the wonderful totality of our world become so apparent to me as in the moments when I walk through the woods or stand on a mountain peak and am able to witness the awakening of the world – a tiny human being in the structure of the great whole. The smallness that one experiences in these moments, the consciousness of being only a minuscule part of everything – this is a very calming thought for me – just like the time just before our accident, when the car tyre had already lost its grip on the asphalt and we were relentlessly propelled off the road.

The view outside of the emerging world is however only a view. It is precisely in nature that we direct our hearing inwards, listening to our own heartbeat, our own steps, our own movements. In music there have been several attempts to depict nature as a 'painting in notes', in Vivaldi's *Four Seasons* for example, or Richard Strauss's *Alpine Symphony*. They contain impressive effects, of hearing cowbells in an alpine pasture, a rushing waterfall, a gale, a downpour of rain, a hot summer day or a resounding thunderclap. But what music expresses in reality is not the concrete, but merely our perception of nature – our sense of being overpowered, our joy, our fear and our contentment. Nature music is also always art music, which tells us more about the phenomenon of inwardness than about the outward manifestations of nature itself.

In fact, what these wanderings are really about is inner peace. When, at the time of crisis in London, I wandered against the wind on the beach at Bournemouth, I succeeded in attaining a kind of freedom from myself and releasing my thoughts. At that moment something wonderful happened: one no longer thinks actively in old patterns, but can observe one's own brain as it begins to think for itself. How great questions suddenly solve themselves, how gradually an inner peace is attained – and finally leads to a decision. Incidentally, one's walk sometimes seems to depict this process of thought. One no longer stamps or marches, but 'swings' through the world. That was how it was for me on Bournemouth beach, and that is how it is when I walk with my wife, perhaps by the Attersee, or with a friend in the mountains. Then, too, I find the same inner peace. We do not need conversation at such times; it is wandering together that connects us at that moment, as a unit in nature. This is a condition that incidentally also occurs when playing music. Here too, communication takes place without words, since we are all linked together through sound. It is the silence of words that lends wings to the magic of hearing.

III. Markets of music

On the consumption of sound

In praise of boredom

I have no photos from a fitness studio on Instagram, no Facebook posts from my private circle and no tweets wearing bathing trunks. On the podium, too, it is unlikely that the public or critics will catch me breaking into a spontaneous dance. In general, I am more concerned about the effectiveness of the small gesture than a brief second of exceptional attention.

Unfortunately, the classical music business is not that different from other areas of our life. In politics too we have had to deal with a rapid increase in the importance of the attention economy, a concept coined by the philosopher and urban planner Georg Franck which has since taken on a life of its own. 'Attention by other people is the most irresistible of drugs,' Franck writes. 'To receive it outshines receiving any other kind of income. This is why glory surpasses power and why wealth is overshadowed by prominence.' The spiral of attention, meanwhile, demands ever more rapid reactions, with new challenges, arguments and audacious modern crossing of borderlines.

We often say that culture is a reflection of our time, and yet are startled when this really appears to be the case. In fact culture and music are good seismographs, which reflect phenomena – for example populism and the tendency towards flattening. Like the continually new manoeuvres of populist politicians, those fashionable side issues of classicism also move in the same direction: with all the excitement, we are no longer to have time to think. In today's thrill-seeking society, no boredom is allowed, for that could mean that we start to question the light fare which is presented as a shrill and provocative event. Precisely for this reason, I feel it is time to strike up a passionate hymn of praise to boredom:

> Leisure instead of superficial activity
> Contemplation instead of noise
> Reflection instead of distraction

Let others continue shouting, sending out colourful images into the world, and figuring out how to attract even more attention. I would rather give myself over to leisure, read a book, let my thoughts wander, and in this way generate fresh creativity. This continually enables me to find new connections and wide arcs which expand my horizons in my daily musical work.

When I then stand in front of an orchestra again, I try to incorporate these discoveries in my rehearsal work. One of the recommendations I like to make at rehearsals is: 'Please don't force the music on the listeners, but bring people to you. Force the public to listen to you.' Isn't this what it should be about? To make each other sensitive to detail again, to beauty and the depth of silence and the great connections? Doesn't pure effect not only too often cover up nuances, but also dim our view of the whole?

Whether in music or politics, soundbites have instant appeal, what is eye-catching may easily deceive, and populism generates simple categorisations in unchallenging black and white. But what is really exciting is when one is able to reveal to the listener the inner complexities of a masterwork. The approach to art calls for differentiation, subtlety and boundless thirst for knowledge. Every era has its own parameters, and every work of art is subject to the criteria of its time. But this does not mean that one should unthinkingly place oneself above the work of art. Goethe himself knew: 'Actually one only knows when one knows little. Doubt grows with knowledge.' I will never forget a very successful young singer at a rehearsal for Mozart's *Seraglio*. In a disagreement over a tempo, she self-confidently told me: 'Mozart is dead and I am alive!' Mozart was a unique, exceptional genius, and we – however good we are – can never approach his virtuosity as a composer. At best we are talented craftspeople. And any true artist must sometimes doubt himself.

The energy of a performance can stimulate the enthusiasm of an audience, just as other events such as a ski race can carry us away with them. This admittedly does not by any means allow us to conclude that a performance possesses the intensity demanded by the masterwork in question. It can be electrifying and yet miss the central message of the work – or only scratch the surface. For me it is the expression of a populist attitude when an interpretation is aimed at instant appeal and it is merely a question of who can play a work in the most extreme, exaggerated way or achieve greater effects. If a grand gesture is superimposed on nuances, this is often done under the pretext of exhilaration, but this is in the end itself only a hollow effect and merely simulates the essential condition of intimacy. True intimacy in a performance however means that a great closeness exists between the work and the performer, and we as artists are the intermediaries. The point is that musical interpreters should put themselves at the service of the composer, instead of perverting their music as an opportunity for image cultivation. I am not ready to give up my belief that human beings have an inborn longing for real profundity. I am firmly convinced that the deep emotion that music can evoke in us is not to be found on its surface. That which is truly great develops out of intimacy and humility towards the work of art.

We could learn all this from classical music as a lesson for living. But it seems that the economy of attention and the shrillness and volume associated with it have reached the world of music, that the decibelisation of society has already arrived in the marketing of artistic work and the expectations of the public.

What does it say about us, about the public, about society and our understanding of culture if we acclaim the performance of a requiem mass as if we had been listening to a pop concert? Art which no longer has any secrets from us is not art any more, but has been corrupted into trivial entertainment. How often have people told me, after listening to Mahler's 8th Symphony or the Brahms Requiem, that they were 'thrilled'. I would rather wish them to be moved, touched and profoundly affected by the music.

The 'eventisation' and shrill commercial exploitation of classical music and its concerts increasingly unsettle and disturb me. Here I repeatedly encounter the objection that the classical music business should not deteriorate into a museum. But does not this comparison reduce our entire cultural creative work? Are museums not ideal places for masterworks by Tintoretto, Rembrandt, Monet and Picasso, which we contemplate in peace and quiet? Should we, in order to make these works more 'accessible', more 'popular', more 'contemporary', flood them with disco lighting, show them in different colours or even hang them upside down? For myself, I like to go to the Leopold Museum in Vienna to look at the drawings and paintings of one of my favourite artists, Egon Schiele. His painting *The Hermits* (1912), which shows him and Gustav Klimt like two Grim Reapers in long black garments, tells me more about itself every time I see it. I have never 'finished' with it, it keeps drawing me to it, and allows me to discover new aspects of it. It does not need any additions. I just have to engage with it, just because it is simply hanging there.

Populism in cultural life, however, is apparent in so many artists' self-representations, which follow the laws of the marketplace. More and more frequently, it is a question of packaging rather than content, more about the visual than the auditory. Appearance is sometimes not only deceiving, but also seductive! In fact, the music is often ignored, and the spectacular presentation of the person and their displayed emotions are used as a means of promoting their career. Some part of the public also seems to expect exactly this spectacle: the big show, the rapturous reception and the eccentricity. Instead what we really need as answers to our world is the compassion of

Bach, the musicianship of Mozart, or the sensuality of Strauss. Classical music has so much to offer us: from effervescent humour to despairing lament, it spreads out before us the whole emotional palette of which human beings are capable.

What is sad about this development of the spectacle is that unfortunately it has also reached our music colleges. It is no longer only violin, piano, singing and conducting that are taught there. For a long time the curriculum has included self-marketing, self-management and PR in music. All these are certainly important disciplines in our time, and I understand the colleges' reasoning, which is that a perfect musical training on its own is not enough to make a career. But with this concept, are our academies of music not guilty of capitulating to that shrill and hyperactive world in which music should actually be one of the ultimate antidotes? In you come to an amicable solution the end, the calculation is straightforward: if I use 20 per cent of my resources in thinking about my own commercial marketing, only 80 per cent remains for questions of music – and I find that 80 per cent means 20 per cent less time to do justice to the great literature of music.

That musicians today have to keep PR in mind often leads to our forgetting to explore the depths of music. The attention that is to be generated sometimes leads to the misuse of music. And furthermore: when we act as though classical music is an art which can be enjoyed quite simply and thoughtlessly, as casually as a superficial entertainment film in the cinema, we are betraying the public as well as music itself. The cosying-up sales strategy actually represents a lack of respect for Bach, Mozart and Beethoven, for art consists not in general distraction, but in composure.

Even at the time, in 1990, I did not understand it when the 'Three Tenors' believed they could inspire enthusiasm for Puccini and Verdi in the general public with their stadium appearances, as even the great dramaturg and critic Marcel Prawy wrongly believed. I doubt that many people who were intoxicated by the *Vincerò* medley performed by Pavarotti, Domingo and Carreras (which of course is totally legitimate) went the following day to a record shop to buy a complete recording of *Turandot*, let alone a ticket for the opera. On the contrary, the television director Brian Large says now that a monster was created that day, which could not then be tamed. After the concert at the Baths of Caracalla in Rome he was repeatedly asked by the television networks to direct another event as entertaining as the spectacle of the Three Tenors. Mahler's Eighth, Verdi's Requiem? No chance! 'Can't we do another stadium concert?' There was no way back. Arias had suddenly become the circus acts of the media, and people wanted not more opera, but more circus!

I ask myself what concert halls achieve when they woo a young audience and advertise that they can post on Twitter during the concerts. How much can one misunderstand music when mobile phones, of all things, are made acceptable in one of the last places – with the exception perhaps of churches – where they should in good conscience be switched off? How can one open a refuge of inaccessibility so cheaply to the enticements of perpetual accessibility? Is it not slowing down and silence that links a concert hall to a church? Refuges of leisure, from which the excitement of the world is excluded?

The effect of the new shrillness has been noticeable for some time. The hungrier the demands of the market, the more supplies are needed to feed it. In the past, so-called stars of classical music were polished over several years to shine in the heavens for a lifetime. Today their destiny seems to be as a shooting star, rapidly and sensationally burning out. Constellations created to the sound of drums and trumpets have a habit of sinking just as rapidly.

The question of how we can halt this trend is not easy to answer, for it has several quite different causes. One is undoubtedly the need for a quick profit. Artists' careers are like modern technological inventions: telephones used to last for a generation, but today cell phones become outdated within two years. This is lucrative for the manufacturer and may be inevitable for the progress of technological appliances, but classical music is different: timeless and simultaneously not self-seeking.

A further problem of the new classical music market is its staff. Most of the managers and impresarios are more interested in quick money than in the long-term career of their artists. I remember colourful, swashbuckling managers such as Ronald A. Wilford, who worked among others with Claudio Abbado and Herbert von Karajan, Kurt Masur, Riccardo Muti and Yehudi Menuhin, Anne-Sophie Mutter and Mstislav Rostropovich, and singers such as Grace Bumbry, Marilyn Horne and Frederica von Stade. On the one hand, managers like Wilford were ice-cold power brokers, never indifferent to money, as described by Klaus Umbach with such splendid malice in his book *Geldschein-Sonate*. But on the other, Wilford was also a faithful servant to his artists. The business model of a Wilford was not the breathless, brief life cycle of a career and the eternal discovery of young artists, but the relaxed, consistent and evenly paced career path. Classical music was something like the gold standard of music: a market where one had to act with care and attention. The same was true of artistic directors. Ioan Holender, the former director of the Vienna State Opera, was always concerned on behalf of his singers, discovering them in the provinces and promoting them cautiously, but also strictly. Brigitte Fassbaender, after her own career as a singer, took over the Landestheater in Innsbruck and ran it as a house in which she individually and carefully supervised the individual voices. None of them used the tools of the pop industry to work in the classical music market.

Since then, the longing for classical music seems to have become too great to copy the brief and spectacular successes of pop. And so classical music too became shriller, faster and more excited. Greed for profit marked the beginning of the end of the early world of the classics and its benevolent support of artists in their thriving careers.

I know from my own experience how tempting – particularly at the beginning of a career – big promises can be. In my case it was a letter which made me sense that greater things were possible. It was from an agent who wanted to meet me, at the time a 19-year-old provincial nobody. He wanted to take me under his wing. I showed the letter to my teacher, Balduin Sulzer, and he said: 'You have to go!' So I went to meet Andreas Bennigsen in Liechtenstein and immediately became enthusiastic over his plans. I agreed to them, trusted him and listened to his advice. He even persuaded me to change my name, and so Franz Leopold Maria Möst became Franz Welser-Möst. Today I would probably not do this. But I have experienced how close the relationship between an artist and an agent can be when they work together on a plan, follow a path together, when they are linked by music and above all have to trust each other. This even led us to a so-called 'weak adoption', by which a relationship is legally established between the adopter and the adoptee, and all previous genealogical relationships on the adoptee's side remain in place. After seven years of being in business together, during which I had already earned a very good income, I noticed that a large part of Bennigsen's efforts were devoted to money and not to my artistic development. And somehow, the money too was not there any more. All this led to my separation from him.

In the USA, Edna Landau was responsible for my management. I had met her in 1984 and she did a fantastic job of looking after me for 25 years until her retirement. She has become a very close friend, whom I often jokingly call 'my Jewish Mom'. She has always advised me against hasty commitments and preached that 'we will not say yes until you are really ready'. And so she put off my US debut for five years. It finally took place in 1989 in St Louis. This was the beginning of a carefully planned career in America, which culminated in my appointment in Cleveland.

Very young artists run the risk that their great ambition will make them naïve. Their early successes can rapidly mask their inexperience. But the freedom to say no is the real lever enabling them to determine the tempo of their own path. A responsible attitude to this individual freedom is the ultimate sign of a true artistic personality. When young people seek my professional advice, I tell them that they should at an early stage ask themselves an important question. Do they want to make a career for themselves? This is usually very demanding and difficult, and one may possibly have to play according to the rules of the market and continually reassert oneself. Or do they want to become seekers for the rest of their lives, inspiring enthusiasm in others by following their own way? In that case, one must throw one's whole existence into the scales and become aware that a great part of the quest takes place not in the glare of the spotlights but in seclusion. I am of the firm opinion that artists do not define themselves exclusively by charisma – charlatans can do this too – but by their training and knowledge, as well as an endless curiosity. And above all by discipline.

I remember singers like the wonderful tenor Anton Dermota, who from 1966 also worked as a singing teacher. With exemplary discipline, before his appearances he drank only milk with honey, and communicated with his wife only by means of handwritten notes. Today many singers think they can no longer afford such solicitous care for their own bodies, because the market demands more and more from them: recordings, television appearances, book signings, opera evenings and open-air events – all this preferably in one week! There are not many vocal cords, hand tendons or brains which can sustain this circus on a long-term basis. Today it takes a great deal of wisdom and courage, discipline and diligence to create a healthy career. That laziness and luck can also be helpful in a world of hyperactivity is true – but tends to be the exception.

Today there are many good voices, but often training does not match the growing challenges. In addition to this, there is the pressure of the opera houses. The companies become smaller, principal conductors are concerned with their own careers and want as quickly as possible to conduct the major works, and directors proclaim the obsession with youth. A 50-year-old Don Ottavio in Mozart's *Don Giovanni* is almost unthinkable today, and preferably a Salome should, quite authentically, be sung by a 17-year-old soprano. The once valid principle that the theatre is illusion is here ignored. I call this reality mania. By decree of directors, who mostly allow themselves to be guided by visual aspects, it has become very difficult, particularly for young singers, to fulfil expectations and at the same time remain true to themselves.

But it is not only greed and readiness to make use of the music market for quick profit that have increased. The market, at least since the fall of the Iron Curtain, has also exploded and expanded. Competition has grown. Artists have appeared, particularly from Asia and Russia, who in comparison to western European conditions have been trained in much more rigorous environments. To assert themselves in this cut-throat world, more and more young artists desperately seek the quickest vehicle that can take them a few kilometres on their way. Thus we have become an artistic family of freeloading travellers who continually jump on the next bandwagon without knowing where we actually want to go.

For a long-term career, however, it is important to have an actual aim in sight, whether or not one finally attains it. Individual freedom has never been as great as it is today – it is as much a blessing as a curse. It is precisely in a society where so much is possible that it is all the more important to go one's own way. I am convinced that the small gesture, the beauty of silence and the consciousness of what is essential are once again attractive, that in the shrill world of the attention economy we actually yearn for the splendid anachronism of death and shared experience. One of my musicians in Cleveland put this very aptly in a nutshell: 'Music making is not about showing off – it is about sharing!'

Boredom implies pausing for a long time. And this is why I perceive boredom, which is nothing but rejection of the attention spiral, as a particularly exciting form of musical existence.

Quiet, please – Recording

It is no secret that the record industry is in crisis. Between 2017 and 2018, turnover fell from 56 to 42 million euros. A classical music bestseller can today end up on fewer than 10,000 audio media. With small labels, the calculations are as follows: 2,000 discs sold are enough to a great extent to refinance a recording. But it is also true that a large number of classical music CDs can only be sold around 200 to 500 times. So each of these recordings is either a subsidised undertaking, that is, the artists take no fee, or one where they actually lose money. These days even large record companies more and more frequently ask their artists to take on part of the recording costs. This leads to entirely new and sometimes highly creative ideas. The tenor Daniel Behle, for example, finances his recordings traditionally by crowdfunding. In this way he remains artistically autonomous and can realise his own ideas without interference from anyone. Ultimately he uses the label – in this case Sony – merely as a seal of approval and distribution facility.

The fate of the CD industry has in fact long been sealed. On the German-speaking music market, audio streaming has established itself as the highest-grossing format. In 2019 music streams have for the first time overtaken the 100 billion mark with 107 billion released titles. But neither does this method either appear to be a solid business model – except for the streaming providers: Spotify and Co. pay the record companies only a thousandth per cent per stream, and they pass on only a fraction to their artists. At the moment, a way out of this unsatisfactory situation is not in sight. And why should there be? Production continues unabated.

In the audiovisual field, too, streaming is in vogue. Opera houses and concert halls consider it as advertising if their performances are retrievable in people's living rooms. Either they stream to their own portals and offer subscriptions, or they use other streaming portals. Both forms are still in their infancy, since the costs for viewers, compared for example to Netflix, are very high, the choice of products very specialised and the subscription income therefore meagre. All this is far from lucrative. During my time as music director of the Vienna State Opera I found on my desk a statement for one of these broadcasts. I had to laugh out loud when I saw, at the end of a three-page breakdown, the sum of 65 cents.

Thirty years ago things were different; much more money was involved. Thriving business gave the record companies great power over casting in opera houses and at festivals. At the start of my career, record labels were still the promised land for every classical music artist. According to the unofficial rules, if you managed to record with Deutsche Grammophon, Decca or EMI, you had made it. An exclusive contract was something like an order of merit bestowed by the industry.

In the late 1980s, I was approached by Peter Alward, then head of EMI Classics, (Peter went on to run the Salzburg Festival 2010-2016), for which Maria Callas had already recorded, and where Walter Legge, the husband of the soprano Elisabeth Schwarzkopf, was an influential recording producer.

At that time, the end of the record industry's golden era was already in sight. A great musical invention had passed its peak. Enrico Caruso had demonstrated to the world of classical music that a voice recorded on shellac or vinyl could quickly become known throughout the world. The gigantic extent of the conducting careers of Herbert von Karajan and Leonard Bernstein would not have been possible without the record industry. Recordings and television were business models providing princely incomes to artists, orchestras and the labels themselves. Sales of records in the hundreds and thousands were not exceptional.

EMI wanted to produce a Bruckner cycle with me. This was an obvious idea – after all, I come from Upper Austria, just like Anton Bruckner. But at that time I was only 30 years old, and recording a whole cycle seemed presumptuous to me. So I agreed on other projects with Peter Alward. At that time it was a must for a conductor to record Carl Orff's *Carmina Burana* – not least because of the projected sales figures. And indeed our recording (with Barbara Hendricks, by the way) enjoyed very good sales, ringing through the tills more than 150,000 times – a nice supplementary income. But it became increasingly clear to me that it was less a question of supplementary income than of the PR value that such recordings represent for an artist. It amazes me how much the record industry, despite its obvious decline, still clings to old times and its long vanished power. The labels still try to exert an influence over opera houses and television transmissions – and sometimes they even succeed in doing so. In fact, however, the crisis in the record industry has led to sales strategies becoming ever more superficial, so that it is no longer a question of what music is being recorded but what non-musical assets can be deployed to reach the buying public. The CD business has become the accelerant of the PR machine. More and more fanciful stories are told about artists, about their love of animals, their psychological problems, their poverty or their nudity. Only music itself has played an increasingly minor role. This downward spiral seems to continue indefinitely.

The general crisis in the recording industry has also led to the fact that some of the recordings today are horrifyingly badly produced. Both operas and symphonies used to be recorded in studios over a period of days. Today – thanks in part to technological development – it is common practice for concerts to be recorded live and rushed onto the market with all possible speed. The record industry runs at the heels of the event culture and breathlessly depicts it without developing an attitude of its own. No wonder that great orchestras now think twice as to whether they even need a record company. The Berlin Philharmonic have drawn a self-confident conclusion from the present situation and release their music under their own label. The logic behind this is impressive: an orchestra such as the Berlin Philharmonic has many fans throughout the world, and are followed on Facebook alone by almost one and a half million people. No record company could generate that much interest. It is only logical, then, that the Berlin Philharmonic make use of the commitment of their public and fans to sell their own music – both audiovisually in the 'Digital Concert Hall' and physically on conventional CDs.

Despite the sharp decline in the recording business, the great venues have fortunately not lost their attraction for the public, and still represent the greatest source of income. The fact is that CDs and streams no longer exclusively decide the popularity or success of an artist or an orchestra. I am convinced that it is precisely the orchestras today that are well advised to cement their popularity where it originally came into being: at their concerts and in front of their original public. Only when one is on the spot, when one regularly puts one's visions to the test, does one create closeness, enthusiasm and passion. Today all should ask themselves in what parts of the world they want to be famous. For, despite globalisation, the whole world has become much too big for most artists and companies. It is a question of purposefully seeking out markets and serving them wholeheartedly.

One of the most absurd tours of my career was one I undertook in March 1966 with the London Philharmonic Orchestra. We played 18 concerts in 20 days in 16 different cities. This is not only exhausting, but also questionable, since it creates no lasting effect. This is why it was important for me personally to establish regular residences for the Cleveland Orchestra, including one in the Vienna Musikverein. Thanks to the long-term artistic director of this institution, Thomas Angyan, I was able to introduce one of the first residences of an international orchestra in Vienna. This model has been followed by many other orchestras. At that time only seven other orchestras were offered their own cycles in the Golden Hall, but today there are 17 companies who regularly appear here. This is a sign that a real-live concert can most successfully build up the relationship with the audience. And precisely this is a consolation for every serious musician: the authenticity of the orchestra's statement remains the basis of all music-making, and thus of all sales strategies and recordings.

Gugelhupf and three-quarter time

One of my favourite family stories is about my world-famous Austrian ancestors, and here my great-great-grandmother, Katharina Dommayer, who in her day made the headlines as the 'fattest woman' in Vienna, plays a leading role. The Dommayer family was best known for its pastries, and in the mid-19th century ran the 'Casino Dommayer', a dance hall in the Hietzing district of Vienna. The Dommayer line goes back through my paternal grandmother. The marriage of Katharina's daughter Luise linked the Dommayers with the Wild family, the delicatessen dynasty who were equally legendary at the time.

Katharina was apparently a person with a great zest for life. One of her greatest wishes was to see her native city from above. Her son-in-law wanted to do her this favour and ordered a horse-drawn carriage to take her to the top of the Kahlenberg above Vienna, from where there is a beautiful view of the city. However, so the legend tells, because of Katharina's weight the horses began to snort as soon as they began the ascent, and then very quickly went on strike. They lacked the strength to carry my great-great-grandmother up the mountain, and Katharina got out of the carriage in tears. She never did see her beloved Vienna from above.

However, Katharina has entered the history of Viennese pastries as a result of another story. She is credited with the recipe for the legendary Kaiser's Gugelhupf, that delicious cake made with bitter chocolate, walnuts and rum, to which apparently Emperor Franz Joseph was addicted. Once he asked Katharina for the recipe, which she sent to him. The Emperor, who liked to spend the summer holidays in Bad Ischl with his mistress, the Burgtheater actress Katharina Schratt, is said to have passed on the Gugelhupf recipe to the actress. At any rate, my poor great-great-grandmother never got it back. Instead, the Dommayer Gugelhupf passed into Austrian confectionery history under the name of the Schratt Gugelhupf.

I was always entertained by the dark humour of this story, and when the Vienna Philharmonic invited me to conduct the New Year's

Day concert in 2011, I remembered the good Katharina. For more than a year, Clemens Hellberg, the then director of the Philharmonic, and I tinkered with the programme. That year it was obvious that Franz Liszt should be honoured on the occasion of his 200th birthday, but I also wanted to add a personal note to the concert. I was the fifteenth conductor to conduct the New Year's Day concert, and after Clemens Krauss, Josef Krips, Willi Boskovsky, Herbert von Karajan, Carlos Kleiber and Nikolaus Harnoncourt, the seventh Austrian. That was when I recalled Katharina Dommayer and the Casino Dommayer, which was run by her family. Legendary waltz evenings had been held in Hietzinger Hauptstraße (the main street of the district of Hietzing) by Johann Strauss I and Joseph Lanner. In addition, Katharina was the daughter of Johann Georg Scherzer, the manager of the dance hall 'Zum Sperl' in the Viennese district of Leopoldstadt. Here too, waltz history was written, for example in the 'Sperls Festwalzer', the 'Sperl Polka' and 'Sperl Galopp' by Johann Strauss I, and the Ländler folk dance 'Willkommen zum Sperl' (Welcome to the Sperl) by Joseph Lanner.

For the 2011 New Year's Day concert I chose, among others, two pieces by Johann Strauss II, who had made his debut at the Café Dommayer in 1844, aged 19. It was there that he laid the foundation stone for his reputation as the 'new waltz king'. Among others, his 'Debut Quadrille' and 'Amazonen-Polka' rang out for the first time in the Dommayer. And it was my great hope that Katharina would now be able to hear from heaven for the first time how these two pieces sounded at a New Year's Day concert in Vienna.

At the same time, the operetta *Simplicius* by Johann Strauss II, first performed in 1887, was important to me for the programme of my first New Year's Day concert. It was played for the first time at the Theater an der Wien, was a flop (probably because of its admittedly mediocre libretto) and was never really rehabilitated. In the Strauss year of 1899 I performed this work in Zurich and it was recorded on DVD. And so I chose the pieces 'Reitermarsch', 'Donauweibchen'

Franz Welser-Möst added a personal note to the first New Year's Day
concert that he conducted in 2011 with the Vienna Philharmonic

and 'Muthig voran!', all inspired by *Simplicius*, as a framing device
for the first part of the concert.

A presentation such as the New Year's Day concert could easily
be categorised as a gigantic music event. It could however also be
interpreted as part of a musical tradition. In fact, the New Year's Day
concert from Vienna is probably both: an international classical music
event, which is transmitted worldwide in more than 90 countries,
but also an existential quintessence of Austrian musical and social
culture. The true greatness and inner dynamics developed by this
event admittedly become clear only when one is oneself part of it.

The preview concert traditionally takes place on 30 December,
and the so-called 'Silvesterkonzert' on 31 December. On the night of

'Silvester', New Year's Eve, I was lying on the sofa in our apartment at the time in Dorotheergasse, suffering from severe nervous stomach pains. I have probably never been as nervous in my life as I was before that New Year's Eve concert. The difficulties of so-called light music are often underestimated. However, it is the case that with a quite normal orchestral evening one has to deal with perhaps 20 different tempi. With the New Year's Day concert, one has to organise certainly around 200 changes of tempo, which requires of a conductor constant attention and very close dialogue with the orchestra. Every single transition must be constructed, which is nerve-racking for all participants, particularly since the whole world is watching.

When, on the morning of 1 January, I entered the Musikverein, I met Barbara Reit, the presenter for ORF, the Austrian broadcasting company. She must have noticed that I was looking a bit green about the gills. 'That's quite normal,' she said. 'Everyone who appears here for the first time is as white as a sheet before coming on stage.' This, she added, had been true of Nikolaus Harnoncourt, Daniel Barenboim and even Zubin Mehta. Even if one takes in words of comfort like these only as if in a tunnel, they get through and give one courage. The splendid human being and conductor Mariss Jansons, whom I met a few days later at the Vienna State Opera, gave me a big smile and said: 'Only we know how difficult this concert is.'

When, shortly afterwards, the Vienna Philharmonic invited me to repeat the event in 2013, I knew what I was letting myself in for and resolved to enjoy the whole experience rather more attentively. In that year, the world of music was also commemorating the 200th birthdays of Richard Wagner and Giuseppe Verdi, which we added into our programme. Together with the Vienna Philharmonic and Clemens Hellberg, I included on the programme 11 compositions that had never been heard before in a New Year's Day concert, among them Wagner's *Lohengrin* Prelude and an excerpt from the ballet from Verdi's *Don Carlo*.

On criticism and passion

It can hurt, it can offend, it sometimes forces us to think, it can give pleasure – and it is above all necessary. We all need criticism. But for my career I always followed the principle that in the first place it was the orchestra I needed to convince, then the public, and last of all the critics.

From the beginning, my artistic career was accompanied by resistance on the part of the media. During my first time with the Linz Jeunesse Orchestra, negative voices were already mingling in the response from the media. Certainly at the time enthusiasm over these young musicians, who were not overawed by the big challenges of the repertoire, was predominant. My initial youthfully boisterous approach to music in the first stages of my professional life, in Norrköping, Winterthur, Lausanne and in my first guest appearances, was not always only admired. Then, as I have already reported, life took a cruel turn in London.

When I arrived in Zurich, so thoroughly shaken that I had been thinking of choosing another profession, I again experienced a great deal of resistance in the media. Above all, the leading critic of what was perhaps the most distinguished newspaper in Switzerland was not well disposed towards me. Apart from one review – it was of a premiere of *Tannhäuser* – he was invariably disparaging about me. Eventually, the critic's editor in chief concluded that his antagonism to my work must – for whatever reason – spring from a personal aversion, and consequently, from then on, only his fellow critics were allowed to review my performances.

Just imagine a great opera house which has been working for several weeks on a premiere. Singers, conductor, director, choir, musical as well as stage assistants, workshops, stage staff, all have invested their entire energy in the preparation and performance. Towards the end of such a long phase of work there will be great tension, the moment is feverishly awaited when the combined effort can be presented for the first time to the public; even some of the office staff are caught up in the premiere fever. And then, often, with a few strokes of a pen, the whole enterprise is destroyed. When one enters the house on the morning on which the reviews are published, it is always a very special moment. Many have already read what the media have written. Those who have received a hefty share of critical condemnation are comforted, while others are congratulated.

In 2008 I was asked by the artistic director in Cleveland at the time, Gary Hanson, if I would be prepared to give a 'deposition'. Until then I had had no contact with the American legal system and did not know what this meant. The background was that the leading music critic on the local newspaper had repeatedly criticised me very harshly. After six years of these predominantly negative reviews, his employer had replaced him with a colleague. The critic sued him, and also our orchestra. Evidently, I was an important witness in the case. Gary Hanson explained to me in our conversation that a deposition was a statement by a witness which would be made to the critic's lawyer before the trial. To my question as to whether I could refuse, he said, yes, but then the court would serve a summons. Such depositions are recorded on video and transmitted to the judge in question, who then decides whether a trial should take place. After extensive preparation by our lawyer, I undertook two sessions, about six months apart, in the office of the critic's lawyer. The first deposition took five and a half hours, the second two and a half. I found these interrogations very humiliating. The case came to trial, which I was not required to attend, and a jury dismissed every point of the complaint,

How can a difference of opinion over musical visions escalate in such an emotional way? Why do two interpersonal fronts harden so rapidly and apparently insolubly in a cultural debate? How is it possible that Rafael Kubelik, one of the great conductors of the 20th century, should be driven out of his post as musical director of the Chicago Symphony Orchestra after only three years by Claudia Cassidy, the *Chicago Tribune* critic? And how stunned I was when the star Austrian critic Franz Endler, now deceased, explained his understanding of his profession: his role as a critic towards young artists was like the hunter's for wounded game – it must be shot down quickly! The impact is revealed not only by direct criticism. It can in the end implicitly degrade and destroy artists when others are praised to the skies to an immoderate and totally exaggerated extent. And finally, is not total silence on the critic's part a subtle method of discrediting an artist?

On principle I strongly approve of criticism, which should certainly be allowed to be severe and ironic. I am firmly convinced that the love-hate relationship between artists and their critics is an inspiring part of music history. But it should never be disrespectful, whether we are speaking of journalists such as Eduard Hanslick, who once rejected Richard Wagner lock, stock and barrel, or cynical writers such as Heinrich Heine and Friedrich Nietzsche, for whom music always still represented greatness in society, or composers such as Hector Berlioz, whose reviews were as entertaining as they were feared. Not to speak of that Austrian genius of criticism, Karl Kraus, to whom is attributed the wonderful saying: 'Was trifft, trifft auch zu' (roughly, 'If it hurts, it was accurately aimed').

In his song 'Der Musikkritiker' the Austrian chansonnier Georg Kreisler tore a strip off the reviewer's profession. 'Es gehört zu meinen Pflichten, Schönes zu vernichten' ('It's one of my duties to destroy what is beautiful'), he sings, and (not altogether unjustly) 'Denn jedem Künstler ist es recht, spricht man von andern Künstlern schlecht' ('For no artist minds if you speak badly of other artists'). The motivation of the eternally bad-tempered critic, according to Kreisler, is the reviewer's own musical inadequacy. In reality he hates music, and his every word is revenge on musicians or his former music teachers. Although the song is very funny, I believe that exactly the opposite is the case. The occasional skirmish between artists and critics is not based on one or other of them being clueless. That would make things too simple. The tension between the professions consists, I believe, in the fact that for both sides music represents a feeling of the most intimate passion.

For myself, at least, I can claim that music is in the truest sense of vital importance for my life, that I am vulnerable and devoted to my music, and that in it I reveal all intimacy, my attitude to the most important questions for humanity, to love and death, to longing and sorrow. My dreams and nightmares circle around making music. Music simply demands unconditional devotion.

It was important to me to declare to my wife before our wedding: 'Even though I love you above all else, music will probably always come first for me.' I am fully aware of the difficulty of this statement, as is the exceptional circumstance that my wife is able to handle this premise so wonderfully. Without my wife, who knows me intimately, deeply understands me and also accompanies me in word and deed in all my professional ups and downs, it would not be possible for me to carry on my profession as I do. But all my life I have found that nothing means as much to me as those deeply moving moments that I am able to experience in music. In music I have experienced conditions which I could probably never find in 'real life'. At the same time, I thoroughly appreciate my partnership, my friendships and good conversation, but my life is characterised by the fact that music will always take priority for me – a circumstance that is not always easy for people close to me.

Added to this are the physical stresses and strains that professional musicians have to suffer for their art. I do not know any of my colleagues whose bodies have been unaffected by their work. I too am regularly pushed to my physical limits by conducting. I remember appearances with a bone spur in my shoulder in which only mind over matter and strong painkillers could overcome. But absence from rehearsals or performances is not an option – our creative desire for the beauty and greatness of music is too strong.

I am deeply convinced that many of our listeners have a similarly grand passion for music. Listeners, whether audience members or critics, expect answers to existential questions from the interpretations we offer. Any individual who demands such intensive listening should not be surprised if they sometimes feel angered, enraged or personally attacked by our work.

But both with us musicians and our audience there are two further factors which should not be underestimated, which admittedly have little to do with music: vanity and the exaggerated opinion of oneself which sometimes give the impression of someone who thinks they know it all.

As I have said, I am convinced that criticism is vital for the evolution of music. I am however annoyed by the trend of presumed 'objectivisation' of criticism which, particularly since the 1980s, has been a dominant feature of the arts pages. Criticism which deceives its readers into thinking it objective is as absurd as the claim that only one reading of Beethoven's symphonies is acceptable. But music does not offer 'either-or' questions but concurrent or parallel ideas. For me it is important that criticism and critics once again find the courage to make statements that are not formulated at one step removed, but personally, to include the word 'I'. After all, Heinrich Heine and Friedrich Nietzsche are already characterised by their radical subjectivity. The word 'I' in a review would also simplify the conflict between artists and critics. We should not see ourselves as facing an imaginary court hearing, but the opinion of an individual who is enthusiastic about music. The critic would then be an intellectual partner, with whom one could have a passionate debate about parallel interpretations, with a unifying devotion to the same subject – music.

It would also be absurd to believe that on account of a review I would conduct in a completely different way the following day. On the evening of a performance, I already have several weeks behind me during which I have intensively engaged with the score, have exchanged notes with the musicians and tested the practicability of my ideas in rehearsal. It would be quite impossible to follow a completely different concept on the next day after reading a damning review.

No artist wants to be booed. We practise our art to inspire and delight people, not to disappoint them. I remember an appearance

The ambition to create a perfect sound
is greater than the need for applause

with *Fidelio* in 1991 at the Deutsche Oper Berlin. At the end of the
performance I went in front of the curtain and for the first time in
my life found myself facing a gigantic wall of people booing. I had
no idea what was happening and was completely bewildered. I could
not understand the rage that was being expressed. Next morning, the
artistic director, Götz Friedrich, summoned me: 'Dear Herr Welser-
Möst, here the artists are not engaged by the audience or the press,
but by the artistic director!' For the rest of my life I will be grateful
to this great man of opera for his words of comfort, especially since I
later found out that the protest was not at all to do with the musical
side of the evening, but about personal intrigues, concerning a dispute
between Götz Friedrich and the conductor Giuseppe Sinopoli, in
which I had become involved merely by my presence. At the time,

however, that concert of booing showed me how difficult it is to hold out against such emotionally concentrated opposition.

It almost seems to have become a ritual to boo directors at the end of a premiere. I was present, for example, when Claus Guth's highly interesting and passionately elaborated production of *Fidelio* was booed at the 2015 Salzburg Festival – and at the first night party I saw how deeply hurt and unnerved he was. But as hard as it may be to handle at the time, the booing can certainly be understood as a kind of distinction, for it also shows that a performance has aroused emotions in the audience, that they have come with individual expectations, and in the end have taken the interpretation of an evening, in terms of music and staging, very personally. All this is very understandable, since what is involved is something very intimate, namely the deepest of feelings. Sometimes I ask myself how often someone engages in such intimate moments with other people as during a concert or an opera. This too is something of which we artists should be aware: that, with our work, we come almost shamelessly close to the emotional landscapes of our listeners.

Music after all is not only a 'philosophy in sounds', of which I like to speak; it is also always intuitive, and touches us directly and in the truest sense of the word. Music can get under our skin. It can overwhelm us. This is a fragile and vulnerable condition which is much too often underestimated.

There are many different ways to listen. There is the distracted listener, the reveller, the co-conductor, and then there is the one who, in the course of a concert, completely forgets space and time and finds himself in the middle of the music, surrounded by sound. Once, during a concert by the Gustav Mahler Jugendorchester (with which I worked as an assistant conductor in its early years) in Paris, with Anton Webern's Six Pieces for Orchestra, Op. 6, I saw the great Pierre Boulez sitting in front of me. Claudio Abbado was conducting. Only a second after the last note had resounded, Boulez turned to his companion in the seat next to him and whispered: '112 mistakes!' To this day I ask myself if listening with a compulsive search for mistakes cannot also be a burden.

At the end of a performance the audience has the right to be troubled, to be furious, and even to boo. This is something we conductors, as well as the directors, have to expect. But much more overwhelming than applause for us musicians is the silence after the last note. I experienced this once after a performance of Beethoven's Fifth Symphony with the Cleveland Orchestra in Hamburg. After the last note, there it was, that state of being out of this world, the moment in which time stands still. No applause. Not a peep from the audience. The absolute silence of wonder as a moment in eternity. As a moment in which feelings are so confused that they need to be restored to order. I do not know how long the silence lasted until applause broke out. But I know that such moments are very special and rare.

Applause pleases all artists, but more important to me is the longing for perfection of sound. I must confess that as an artist one can become addicted to musical moments in which the intoxication of silence suddenly becomes pervasive.

It is however also important to have phases of rest, to take a step back, so as not to become worn down by the addiction to sound. For this reason, since 1995 I have acquired the habit, after living almost entirely out of a suitcase for ten years, of regularly making time for leisure and collecting myself. Whenever I go on holiday I need at least ten days before the 'inner sound tape' in my head stops playing the music of the past weeks.

The emotional power of music cannot be underestimated – neither its power over musicians nor its power over the public and the critics. Music touches our most intimate feelings, and leaves us vulnerable. And perhaps this very realisation can help us put whatever the disputes are about the art of sound, onto a more stable foundation.

Third journey

Spirit of silence

I like to go into retreat. And I am glad to have been in a position to plan and build my own refuge space: my library, which stands behind our house on the Attersee. A large square house with books – belles lettres, non-fiction, philosophy – and musical scores. All this on two levels, with an aisle whose sides are connected in the middle by a sort of bridge. The only items of furniture are a large wooden desk and a seating area by the window, as well as a rare old piece that I inherited from my grandmother, a Werkl – the predecessor of a record-player. On the walls, alongside contemporary artworks, are pictures of my ancestors and a family tree drawn up by my father. Nothing else.

Libraries have always had a magical attraction for me, whether Baroque wooden reading rooms with turned spiral staircases in old monasteries or ultra-modern national libraries like the one in Paris. They are spaces filled with knowledge, places where people whisper. They offer us shelves full of possibilities for concentration and contemplation. I have always venerated the profound knowledge to be found in good books. When, ten years ago, in a coffee house in Vienna, I told the legendary critic Karl Löbl of my plan to build a library, he replied succinctly: 'That is the difference between you and someone who would spend the same money on a Ferrari.'

Indeed, I also travel in my library, though not in the same way as I would in a fast car. I travel through the ages, from the meditative monks of the Middle Ages to the visionaries of postmodern society, through a variety of genre landscapes, from the glossy high-rise world of financial theory via the philosophy of a Marcus Aurelius to a picture book about the world of mountains.

In a library, time and space disappear, and everything can be connected with everything else, totally free and totally analogous: the operas of Richard Strauss with Greek classical antiquity, the operas of Mozart with the works of Voltaire and Rousseau, the 'spherical shape of time' in an opera such as Bernd Alois Zimmermann's *Die Soldaten* with the *Confessions* of St Augustine and Heidegger's *Being and Time*, and the symphonies of Gustav Mahler with the theories of Sigmund Freud on psychoanalysis.

Sometimes I particularly enjoy, quite by chance, encountering cross-connections, for example when I recently read an essay by the American art critic Clement Greenberg. From the 1930s Greenberg was the most influential supporter of Abstract Expressionism. As early as 1989 he wrote this sentence which impressed me greatly: 'Effect becomes content, replacing substance.' Is this not a condition which pertains once again to the classical music scene of today?

All this could sound as though I were a hermit or even a misanthrope, which certainly is not the case. I have always observed Herbert von Karajan with wonder, standing in the Musikverein looking lost and lonely, although surrounded by so many people. At such times it has become clear to me how lonely one can be even in the society of others, and I have never wanted to build a career at such a cost.

I distinguish rather sharply between the conductor Franz Welser-Möst as a public person and myself as a private person. At public appearances, at receptions or balls, I have developed a defence mechanism. I am of the strong opinion that small talk does not justify amicable intimacy, so that in such cases I tend to adopt a friendly but non-committal manner – solely to protect myself and my wife. At the same time, however, we cultivate very intensive and long-lasting friendships, many of which go a long way back.

I believe two things are important for our profession: the authenticity of friendship which is not devalued by the superficiality of the jet set, and the possibility of retreat into the silence of contemplation. In my case, apart from walking in nature, it is the path through my library that best leads me to myself. I fear that many people have forgotten how to engage intensively with things, to submerge and sink into new thoughts. The enticements of pervasive distractions are too great. Here too I believe in the doctrine of the mean, but there is one thing that I consider existentially important at all times. Whatever one happens to be doing at the time, one should do it with all due devotion and concentration – in life as well as in music.

IV. Artists and music

On the production of sound

Learning from legends

Neither my teacher Balduin Sulzer nor I have ever liked the idea of competitions. But the conductors' competition that Herbert von Karajan created in Berlin as long ago as 1969 seemed exciting to me. And so, with youthful insouciance, I registered as a participant in 1979. After a few rounds, I suddenly, aged just 19, found myself in the finale. Before the last round, Albert Moser, at the time general secretary of the Vienna Musikverein and a member of the jury, came to me and told me that I was considered 'very gifted', but that I must understand that I was 'much too young' to receive a prize. This hit me at the time like a kick in the stomach.

It is often forgotten how much Karajan cared about young talent. Mariss Jansons and Valery Gergiev were winners of his conductors' competition, and it was he who discovered and encouraged musicians such as Anne-Sophie Mutter and made them well-known. Now he was suddenly standing in front of me. I remember his smart camel-hair coat and his grey combed-back hair. Karajan, 71 years old at the time, said to me: 'Whenever you want – come to my rehearsals. And if I can do anything for you, just call me.' When I asked him which college he would recommend to me for my studies, he replied that Munich or Berlin would be best for my professional advancement.

In the end I decided against studying in Berlin and in favour of Munich, because the geographic closeness of the latter to Linz would enable me to continue running my Jeunesse Orchestra. During my studies I used every free minute to attend the rehearsals and performances of great conductors. Today, when young students come to me, I often ask them what productions they have seen in recent weeks. Some of them reply: 'I have had no time to attend productions, my studies keep me so busy that I simply don't manage it.' I cannot understand this attitude. To soak up music, to observe other conductors at work – could there be a more exciting and important study?

In my own case, I certainly took my teaching at the music college seriously in most of the subjects, but the opportunity to be able to watch other conductors at work was at least as important to me. I enjoyed my freedom during my studies, and can state that without doubt my teachers between 1980 and 1984 were not only the professors at the Munich music college, but also, indirectly, the great conductors Leonard Bernstein, Sir Georg Solti, Sergiu Celibidache, Bernard Haitink, Carlos Kleiber and Wolfgang Sawallisch.

There are many legends about Karajan. The one that relates that he was a master at cultivating his own image is certainly true. The maestro who conducted his orchestra with eyes closed became a sort of trademark. But at rehearsals Karajan was a very meticulous and painstaking musician, who above all else excelled at conveying his thoughts perfectly to an orchestra.

What particularly fascinated me was the clarity and unrivalled efficiency of his work. With one movement Karajan could completely change the sound of the orchestra. I remember a rehearsal for a Bruckner symphony. Herbert von Karajan demanded of the violins a tremolo of maximum speed and excitement. He stopped the orchestra with a wave of his hand, looked up briefly and said: 'Have you ever stepped into a wasps' nest?' Then he continued to conduct and immediately got what he wanted: a wonderfully agitated humming and buzzing. In short, Herbert von Karajan was a miracle of efficiency!

But he could also be combative. At the rehearsals for *Lohengrin* at the 1984 Easter festival in Salzburg, I was sitting, at his invitation, directly behind him in the Great Festival Hall. This was at the time when the tensions between the great old man and the Berlin Philharmonic were already becoming noticeable. At one of these rehearsals he wanted the violins to quickly perform a *fortepiano* with a stroke of the whole bow. This was followed by tumult – it was the classic spark that caused the powder keg to explode. What a scene! Orchestra members sprang from their seats and screamed at Karajan, while he sat there, stony-faced. I tried to make myself as small as possible in my seat. When the noise had died down, Karajan said, in a voice of admirable calm: 'Does this mean that in future we will have to take a vote on whether to play *piano* or not?'

To this day I am baffled as to how he and the world-famous orchestra could continue to play after this scene, not only highly professionally, but also with the most beautiful Wagner sounds imaginable. I should therefore also mention that in rehearsals and performances the Berlin Philharmonic always gave Karajan what he wanted in terms of sound – even in this late phase, when in many areas there was already personal friction between him and the orchestra. For both sides, the music was more important than the interpersonal conflict.

Ultimately, however, Karajan was also a master of psychology. Just before Whitsun of the same year he was in Vienna, recording Vivaldi's *Four Seasons* in the Hofburg with Anne-Sophie Mutter and the Vienna Philharmonic. The Salzburg Whitsun Festival was close at hand. Three concerts by the Berlin Philharmonic had been arranged, with Lorin Maazel, Seiji Ozawa and Herbert von Karajan, and myself as reserve conductor. The row between Karajan and the Berliners was at its peak, and he had withdrawn his invitation to them for his concert in Salzburg and instead invited the Vienna Philharmonic. For the first part he had put *The Four Seasons* with Anne-Sophie Mutter on the programme, and for the second part Johannes Brahms' First Symphony, for which only one rehearsal, on Whit Sunday in the Vienna Musikverein, had been arranged. I was able to watch this fascinating rehearsal too, from a box near the stage. Karajan rehearsed only the parts of the symphony which were apparently important to him, and after 45 minutes he said: 'Thank you, gentlemen!' This was the master psychologist in action. By not having the whole symphony played through, he was conveying to the musicians his unbounded confidence, in the knowledge that they would give their all at the concert. Gerhart Hetzel, the orchestra leader, and other musicians leapt up and begged, indeed demanded of him that an acoustic rehearsal should be held in Salzburg on the morning before the concert. Karajan said placidly: 'But you know the acoustics of the Great Festival Hall.' However, he then quickly allowed himself to be 'persuaded'. I do not know if I have ever in my life heard a more intensively played performance of Brahms' First Symphony. In this highly fraught situation of competition with their Berlin colleagues, the Vienna Philharmonic mustered all the beauty of sound and musical passion of which they are capable.

After the Karajan era, the Berlin orchestra embarked on a new future. It is probably an inevitable part of the development of great institutions that they must symbolically kill their father figures to become free. Thus it was only logical that Herbert von Karajan should be succeeded by his antithesis: Claudio Abbado became principal conductor of the Berlin Philharmonic. On his first entrance he greeted the orchestra, until then strongly hierarchical and conductor-oriented, with the revolutionary words: 'Hello, I'm Claudio.' The contrast could not have been greater.

I was able to assist Claudio Abbado from 1985 to 1986, when, after his time at La Scala, Milan, he became general music director in Vienna. Abbado was known as a non-rehearsing conductor; he relied – often with justification – on his ability to infuse a performance with life and fire on the night. What particularly impressed me about him was his attitude to the supposedly irreverent in music. Abbado made it unmistakably clear that he took every note seriously, even the slightest pizzicato accompaniment of the second violins. For him there was no such thing as a continuous rubato or a blurring of contours. Not even for world stars did Abbado make an exception. When, at a rehearsal of *Un ballo in maschera*, Luciano Pavarotti wanted to hold a high note for the sake of the effect, Abbado, standing in the pit, flagged down the orchestra and the tenor with the severity of a traffic policeman. It was a magnificent thing to watch.

Incidentally, in my youthful impetuousness I actually took Herbert von Karajan up on his offer to let me call him when I needed help. I had applied for the post of general music director in Ulm, where of course Karajan's career had also begun. At the time it was my dearest wish to work in opera, a wish which was not fulfilled until 12 years later in Zurich. So I thought he might be able to help me. It took a huge effort on my part, but then I rang the porter at the Hotel Kempinski in Berlin, where Karajan used to stay, and was put through to him. Nothing came of my application, but later I learned that Karajan actually rang the mayor of Ulm on my behalf, which I still find surprising today.

The individual and power

There are quite different types of role model, the great world-famous stars, but also those who arouse one's enthusiasm and influence one in a personal and direct way. Among my models of this kind were Balduin Sulzer, but also a conductor such as Kurt Wöss, who took over the running of the Bruckner Orchestra in Linz in the late 1960s, and appeared with them in the newly opened Brucknerhaus. Previously the orchestra had performed in a sports hall. The life story of Kurt Wöss is interesting: his career began, not uncontroversially, during the Nazi period. After the war he first directed the Tonkünstler Orchestra in Lower Austria, and in the 1950s he went to Tokyo as the first principal conductor of the NHK Symphony Orchestra, and became one of the first pioneers of classical music in Japan. I remember many wonderful concerts with him, and for me he incorporated the type of the *grand seigneur*. I also have vivid memories of concerts with the young, exuberant Theodor Guschlbauer, the general music director in Linz during my time at the Musikgymnasium. Both he and Wöss were passionate in their aim of bringing an understanding of high-quality music to a regional public.

On the international stage, too, it is interesting to observe that the history of music is marked, often at the same time, by very antithetical personalities, characters which seem to span between them the extremes of a *zeitgeist*. Here I think of a pair such as Wilhelm Furtwängler and Arturo Toscanini – they were not only politically, but also aesthetically, complete opposites.

After the war, a similar constellation was formed by Herbert von Karajan and Leonard Bernstein. Karajan was a jetsetter, a marketing genius, a pioneer of performing operas in the original language, and – as I have already described – a pedant in his work with an orchestra. Leonard Bernstein, on the other hand, was in addition a brilliant composer. He stood for intellect, but also for hedonistic self-indulgence, for a mixture of Apollo and Dionysus, though tending more towards the latter. Perhaps the best title for this exceptional artist is that of the 'I-musician'. He was a genius who created his own cosmos and opened up completely new worlds, for example that of Gustav Mahler. Bernstein revolutionised the reception of Mahler's music. As a student I had often heard *Zarathustra*, *Till Eulenspiegel* and other tone poems by Richard Strauss, but Mahler's symphonies were then still considered 'cheap' and 'emotional kitsch'. Bernstein liberated Mahler for the world of music from these absurd accusations, and in doing so opened up a wide field in which we still move today with great enthusiasm.

During my student time in Munich I was also able to observe Leonard Bernstein at work a few times, for example at rehearsals of the legendary concert performances of *Tristan and Isolde*, with the Symphony Orchestra of the Bayerischer Rundfunk. It was fascinating to study his charisma. It was not just his casual manner, his dancing, laughing demeanour. He convinced the orchestra much more with his boundless learning. He explained the origin of sound to the wind players while incidentally quoting from Goethe's *Faust*, and wandered through the history of music in the course of his explanations. The best thing about him was that he never used his knowledge to give an academic lecture, it was simply present, and entertaining stories kept bubbling out of him. There is probably no more fascinating combination than that of emotionality and knowledge. But in Leonard Bernstein there was also an amusing contradiction. Once, after a clearly very long and very lively evening, he came to a rehearsal of one of his own symphonies. After a relatively short time he looked at the orchestra, ran his fingers through his hair, laughed and then said in a hoarse, hangover-laden voice: 'Sorry, now I have even forgotten my own music. You'd better go home!'

Perhaps Sergiu Celibidache is a missing member of the Karajan–Bernstein constellation. He too was a conductor whose work I was often able to experience repeatedly when I was a student in Munich. At that time he was principal conductor of the Munich Philharmonic. Celibidache presented himself completely differently from Herbert von Karajan. The latter's arrival was certainly recognisable from the large entourage which always surrounded him. Karajan himself however often sat quite alone and self-absorbed in the corner of the hall. Celibidache on the other hand filled every hall simply by entering it. The Munich Philharmonic were totally controlled by his persona; they were a purely 'Celi-Orchestra'. And this 'Celi' took whatever he needed for is art, for example some 12 rehearsals for each new programme. Sergiu Celibidache was a brilliant circus ringmaster, an animal trainer. If Herbert von Karajan can be called a magician of sound, Celibidache was perhaps a master of the musical autopsy. He exposed every single nerve fibre of a score, sometimes admittedly at the expense of the liveliness of his interpretation.

Celibidache as a rule rehearsed at high volume and without consideration of anyone who floundered. He had no problem in showing up an individual musician. At the start of every piece, the copper bracelets he had been given by some shaman rattled on his arm, and he enjoyed playing psychological games with the orchestra. I was present at the rehearsals for Anton Bruckner's Fourth Symphony when he greeted the orchestra with a grumpy 'Good morning', sat on his chair, raised his baton, then lowered it, at the same time shouting 'TOO LOUD!' The second violins and the violas had not yet played a single note. This too is a way of demanding a tremolo, a collective spasm, from the orchestra.

Celibidache is often celebrated for his interpretations of Bruckner. But I was more impressed with his conducting of other composers. With Bruckner's works I often feel that he is conducting two slow movements and one very slow movement. I liked Celibidache much better when he was creating colour in sound, with Ravel or Debussy for example.

Whether it was Bernstein, Karajan or Celibidache, we were dealing with a generation of conductors who liked to think of themselves as figures of authority – a type of musician which probably should include Kurt Masur, who is said to have ruled in highly dictatorial style in Leipzig. I find it strange when orchestras today still want to be conducted by such domineering personalities. As a rule, these are individuals who impose their style without ifs or buts, who say exactly how they want things, and whom one can follow with one's brain switched off. I believe that this state of affairs, particularly today, cannot end well, because this would mean disconnection from society. Making music today can only be done in a spirit of togetherness.

In his excellent book *Crowds and Power*, Elias Canetti dedicated a whole chapter to the profession of the conductor. He wrote it with the Second World War and the Nazi dictatorship in mind, and to him the conductor was a manifestation of power, continually threatening and ice-cold at heart. 'There is no more obvious expression of power than the performance of a conductor,' he wrote. The conductor is 'an almighty guardian of sound and silence' an autocrat who has carte blanche to do what he wants, a ruler over the orchestra and the

The conductor is a servant, not a master: Franz Welser-Möst in
Cleveland rehearsing *Ariadne on Naxos*

audience in equal measure. Sergiu Celibidache would probably have
agreed with Canetti, for after all it was he who said that conductors
are actually 'dictators', who 'fortunately are content with music'.

This topic has repeatedly preoccupied me in the course of my
various positions. A special case in the Western orchestral world is
represented by the system in Cleveland, where the music director has
a singular degree of power. He has total personal sovereignty, that
is, he alone ultimately decides, after the audition and subsequent
consultation with a committee of musicians, who will be accepted
in the orchestra. I listen very carefully to the arguments presented
during these consultations, but my decision is then a lonely one. This
loneliness makes the responsibility I bear all the greater. For a top

team like that in Cleveland it means not compromising in matters of staff, for a compromise ultimately always remains a compromise. Every decision must be taken with the aim of raising the artistic standard. The guidelines for a new appointment are of course the command of the instrument at the highest level, the musicality of a *Kammermusiker* (a distinguished instrumentalist) – that is, the ability to listen constantly to the other musicians combined with the highest vigilance – and the readiness to take one's place in this collective and subordinate oneself to the aims of the institution.

As the holder of a leading position I have to be there for the others and not expect to be served by them. An old Italian proverb says: 'The king is the first servant of the people.' The conductor too should define himself as a servant and not a ruler. My understanding of power means that I put myself at the service of the institution. But the most important thing for me is respect for all who work with me and who contribute with their abilities and manpower to the realisation of common goals. Respect is based on reciprocity, and can only be demanded if one is oneself ready to bestow it on others. An expression of misuse of power is accordingly lack of respect. As a conductor, it would be all too easy – in view of the musical complexity that we face in a score – to show up an individual musician and put him in a bad light. Sometimes one might want to do this to cover up a mistake of one's own. The temptation to do so is great, and one's ego is only too ready to lead us into it. But no conductor will lose face as a result of apologising for a mistake.

For me, the authority of a conductor consists first and foremost in the persuasive power of conviction of his knowledge, and can only have the purpose of arousing enthusiasm in the orchestra and audience for their common listening experience. I would sum it up as follows: ideally, conductors work together with an orchestra to enable the statement of a work to be heard. It is not a question of making a decision about something, but about persuading an orchestra through knowledge. It is also not a question of issuing instructions to the respective sections, but to listen – that is, to shape the sound offered by the musicians. Making music is dialogue and respect for the craft of others. Therefore the conductor's basic attitude must be: 'I can't play the oboe, but I have an idea as to how a musical phrase can be played.'

As a rule, orchestras are very quick to notice if a conductor knows the piece, if he has something to say and if he will and can work together with the orchestra. In the early years of my career I found with several orchestras that the musicians tested me in a crass and ill-mannered way. Some tried to throw me off balance with provocative remarks or by persistently glaring at me. This was at a time when some orchestras thought that a young conductor should begin by going through the fire of personal attacks. Happily, these times are over.

Creating art together is a deeply emotional matter. And, sooner or later, tensions are bound to emerge. No conductor is spared. My credo is that openness should be preserved in teamwork. And I believe it is important to address problems before they get out of control. There are always things that should not happen which, in the heat of conflict, just do happen. Sometimes it is just a misunderstanding that makes a mountain out of a molehill – especially when an individual challenges the basic confluence of the whole. Both physical and emotional misbehaviour – in whatever form – are unacceptable.

At this point I would like to digress briefly on the subject of female conductors in the orchestra world. A few decades ago, they were not yet welcome in orchestras. This has changed for the better. As in so many other areas of our society, it is an overdue development that renowned orchestras are increasingly led by women. It is discrimination, plain and simple, when women at the conductor's stand are still seen as exceptions, and their performances judged by other criteria than those of their male colleagues. Prejudice and distinction are always discriminatory. Nevertheless, it is unfortunately the case that the debate about equal opportunities for men and women in the world of the arts still continues to flare up here and there, and is conducted with the spurious arguments which lay emphasis on gender difference. Only when this debate is over can we be sure that male and female conductors will be judged exclusively according to artistic criteria, and that the topic will thus resolve itself.

From my workshop I: Beethoven's Ninth

The conductor's job is a lonely one. In what follows, I would like to give some insights into my conducting workshop. Before the work is performed, there is a long lead time, an intensive period of preparation and a deepening confrontation with the score and the cultural background of the work.

I have chosen Beethoven's Ninth Symphony as an example in this book, because to me it is a key work in musical history. Beethoven was the first composer whose music requires the listener not to be entertained, but to be shaken to his innermost being, to participate emotionally and be challenged. In this respect, this symphony represents a high point – a composition with an elevating spirit in philosophical and musical terms.

A cultural giant such as Beethoven must be approached from many sides for the purpose of interpretation. Many books have been written about this monument of Western culture. A small insight may provide a sense of the overwhelming greatness of this work.

The development of an interpretation can be compared to the solving of a puzzle. One piece of information is added to another until finally as complete a picture as possible is formed. To celebrate this symphony as the high point of classical music would fall far short. It is a musical and philosophical statement which, formed from the spirit of classicism, is already moving towards Romanticism, looks back to the past and points to the future. It transcends time and is timeless.

Everyone knows the famous melody of the 'Ode to Joy', 'Joy, beautiful spark of divinity, Daughter from Elysium', on which the

Anthem of Europe is also based. Before this melody rings out from all members of the orchestra in the fourth movement of the Ninth, Beethoven takes us on an extended musical and emotional journey. What does this journey look like? A letter by the composer of 1812 to a friend, a little girl in Hamburg who was 10 years old and named Emilie, serves us as a guide: 'Go on, don't only practise art but get at the very heart of it; it deserves that, because only art and science can truly put humanity in touch with divinity.'

In this way, Beethoven in this work confronts death, hope and the victory of the human spirit over all the difficulties of life. In the first movement of the Ninth he begins with a dead void, musically represented by the tonal uncertainty of a fifth, which becomes increasingly charged with rhythm, harmony and motif, and rises up to the mighty first theme. This reminds me of the beginning of the sixth *Hymn to the Night* by Novalis, with the heading 'Longing for death':

> Into the bosom of the earth,
> Out of the Light's dominion,
> Death's pains are but a bursting forth,
> Sign of glad departure.

Novalis, the original Romantic, had already been dead for 23 years when the Ninth was first performed in 1824. A central motif of Romanticism is longing. Following the first theme in the first movement Beethoven allows us to experience this longing in terms of sound – first with a brief bridge passage, in which a melody resounds expressive of the yearning for brotherhood. This is followed by the second theme, which, beginning with a musical sigh and symbol of Christ, allows us to sense what Beethoven wants to express. Let us again quote his own words. From his letter to the *Immortal Beloved* of 1812: '… and when I regard myself in connection with the universe, what I am, and what he is — whom one calls the greatest — and yet — here is again the divine spark of man.' Under the influence of the philosophy of German Idealism, Beethoven increasingly moves humanity closer to the divine.

Beethoven concludes the first great section of the first movement with a musical statement which is reminiscent of the struggle of the Enlightenment for liberty, equality and fraternity. Just before the end of this movement, whose theme is the question of death and victory over death, the composer gives us a brief glimpse of a better world. Suddenly, and totally unexpectedly, the horns play a small fragment of the first theme, but bathed in a beautiful, warm and pleasant light. It is as though, in the course of this journey, after the dramatic first part and the warlike confrontation with all the difficulties of life, with death in sight, he wants to show us the aim of our existence.

The second movement is marked as a scherzo. This term usually denotes a playful, light-hearted piece of music, and characterises a fast dance movement. But there is nothing playful to be observed here. Like the first movement, it is in the key of death, D minor. Beethoven opens out before us a grim dance of death which reminds me of some of the paintings of Egon Schiele. What is happening here is marked by dynamic, wild extremes. The central section, the trio, represents a great atmospheric contrast to the scherzo, whose power is hardly surpassed in musical history. The trio creates a rural idyll of sound inspired by Beethoven's Pastoral Symphony. It evokes the same sunlight as the brief glimpse of the aim of human existence epitomised by the sound of the horns at the end of the first movement. Immediately after this idyll, Beethoven again plunges us into the struggle for survival with a repetition of the dance of death.

I can only speculate as to why Beethoven diverges from the order of movements in the classical symphony and places the scherzo in second place in the series of four movements. With Haydn, Mozart and also in the preceding eight of Beethoven's symphonies, it was usual to place the slow movement after the first, and the dancing passage of the scherzo or minuet in third place. I believe that Beethoven wanted to extend the sense of emotional fall as much as possible. After the

In 2017 Franz Welser-Möst and the Cleveland Orchestra linked the music of Beethoven with an educational project for young people in the *Prometheus Project*

drama of the first movement, the emotions are further whipped up by the dance of death in the second. The relief of tension and reflectiveness that follow only in the third movement are a stroke of genius. This particularly intensifies the depth of the slow movement in its intended effect.

The third movement begins with musical sighs, which prepare us for the first great dying away of the melody. The beginning of the melody again allows us to hear the musical symbol of Christ, but in contrast to the first movement, the melody does not rise, but descends: Christ is descending towards us with a message of hope. This is embodied in the key of B flat major, in which this movement is composed. Beethoven takes us on a journey which feels like a kind of meditation. Each of the musical ideas of the first movement is echoed by an added repetitive phrase, as though he wishes to dwell on a beautiful image in his imagination. The second theme is in the sunny key of D major, which also marks the brief glimpse at the end of the first movement and in the trio of the second.

This key represents the aim and symbolises the victory of the human spirit, which finds fulfilment only at the end of the symphony. A melody which seems to have no beginning and no end denotes the persistence of the longing of mankind in the meantime. Beethoven holds the melody, adorns the first theme with variations and gives it further depth. Then a second theme rings out. He clothes this in a gentle light, as if he wishes to express that the yearning of mankind for its aim is a childlike notion. Next, the first musical theme is deepened in an even more ornate variation. Beethoven makes it flow directly into a motif presented with loud trumpets and timpani, derived from the Freemasons' initiation ritual. The message? That the human spirit is free and independent!

This passage reminds me of Johann Wolfgang von Goethe's hymn 'Prometheus':

> Here sit I, forming mortals
> After my image;
> A race resembling me,
> To suffer, to weep,
> To enjoy, to be glad,
> And thee to scorn,
> As I.

In my opinion Beethoven here wanted to equate Christ with the figure of Prometheus. In the period of the Enlightenment, the figure of Prometheus symbolises everything of which mankind is capable. As in the letter cited earlier, and also recognisably in other writings and notes by Beethoven, the idea of the divine in man takes a central role in his artistic legacy. This is the source of Beethoven's will to change in the world, to the moral purification of the individual, to the absolute demand for freedom and community with all mankind. Like philosophy, Beethoven's music aims at the universal, at the great themes of politics, nature, religion, death and life. With the prospect of a possible, ideal world, mankind can gain a deep understanding of happiness and freedom.

The slow third movement ends with the sighing motifs with which it began, and, right at the end, with a 'farewell' motif, as if he needed to say farewell to all his thoughts about humanity and contemplation.

But he would not be the titan Beethoven if he were satisfied with this.

At the beginning of the fourth movement he assaults us with a shout of chaos, dissonance, despair, to which E. T. A. Hoffmann refers in his critique of this symphony: 'Beethoven's music sets in motion terror, fear, horror, pain and awakens the infinite yearning that is the essence of romanticism.'

This strident outcry is followed by a passage that is entrusted in the manner of a recitative to the low-pitched string instruments. It tells us what the human singing voice will later express in verbal form: 'Oh friends, not these sounds! Let us instead strike up more pleasing and more joyful ones!'

On the occasion of the first performance, Beethoven noted that the recitative should be played 'beautifully'. This suggests that beauty was an important and much discussed artistic concept in his day, which may perhaps be surprising with this revolutionary of classical music. We also know this from statements and entries in the conversation notebook which he needed to keep on account of his increasing deafness, in order to communicate with others.

Following the recitative, Beethoven now allows the low-pitched strings to play for the first time the famous melody 'Joy, beautiful spark of divinity'. This passage is heard in some interpretations in an almost inaudible pianissimo, which is not dramatically justified. Beethoven's intentions are evident in a later note by the composer. When the bass soloist introduces Schiller's famous words about joy, he should do this with a 'pleasing' expressiveness. After the great progression in which ever more instruments join in the song of joy, Beethoven again breaks off the development. He takes us back to the noisy chaos of the beginning, to allow the warning voice of the bass soloist, in view of the threatening darkness, to appeal: "Oh friends, not these sounds! Let us instead strike up more pleasing and more joyful ones!' The dramatic change of mood succeeds. He, the other three soloists and the choir now sing of the joys of the human value of togetherness and friendship. At the phrase 'Even the worm was given desire, and the cherub stands before God', the music forcefully stresses the word 'God'.

There follows a rapid march, in which the 'suns hurtle through the universe', as is heard in the text. Beethoven wrote in a letter of 1814 to Count Franz Brunsvik: 'As regards me, great heavens! my dominion is in the air; the tones whirl like the wind, and often there is a like whirl in my soul.'

In this context, the passage of the ode which ends with the phrase 'joyfully, like a conquering hero' can be understood as the composer's affirmation of his artistry.

But Beethoven also continually astonishes me with his ability to write music about music. Above all in his later creative phase he provides references to the past and cross-connections with his earlier works, and nevertheless points the way to the future like no other. After the rapid march he lets the music loose to us without human voices, a passage paralleled in the spiritual sister of the Ninth Symphony, his Missa solemnis. This represents the terrors of war in musical form. Here in the Ninth Beethoven paints a musical picture of the dark, only to allow, after an exhausted collapse, the exuberant rejoicing of the choir and orchestra at full volume, 'Joy, beautiful spark of divinity', to have an even more tremendous effect.

In the next section of the final movement, which resembles a large-scale cantata, Beethoven goes far back into the past – to the Renaissance, a time in which Greek classical antiquity was rediscovered and also became the basis of the Enlightenment and of classical music. Beethoven devoted himself to the music of the Renaissance masters, and so he links the text 'Be embraced, you millions!' with the musical style of that period. We are dealing here with a sublime concept, transcending time, which places the values of the Enlightenment in a great historical context and reinforces their universal validity.

A note to the passage which follows shortly afterwards: after the words 'Brothers, above the canopy of stars must dwell a loving father' some organ-like bars ring out which Beethoven designates with the tempo marking '*adagio, ma non troppo ma divoto*'. Here another parallel to the *Missa solemnis* can be discerned. At the point when in the Catholic liturgy the bread and wine are transformed into the body and blood of Christ, the music that resounds is similar to that of the Ninth. The thought of the divine Father extends the text into the religious sphere.

The next section, in highly compositional virtuosity, continues to present the themes of joy and the sense of a Father 'above the canopy of stars'. It is reminiscent of Baroque angels singing a great hymn of praise. Although the symphony is not what is called a sacral work, a great spirituality is inherent in it, which can be experienced in such passages.

The last great part of the symphony is staged as a delirium of joy. The magic of joy allows all men to be brothers. In the radiant key of D major, the spiritual sun of the Enlightenment has triumphed over all the darkness of humanity and the material world.

Beethoven, a man of wide reading and culture, must have known the passage from Immanuel Kant's *Critique of Pure Reason*: 'two things fill my mind with ever-increasing wonder and awe, the more often and the more intensely the mind of thought is drawn to them: the starry heavens above me and the moral law within me'. I believe that this quotation brings us very close to the core of the Ninth Symphony: the area of tension between the 'starry heavens' and the moral law defined by man. In his 'Ode to Joy' and its line 'He must dwell beyond the stars' Friedrich Schiller was probably thinking in a similar way. He distinguished between the 'beauty of art' and the 'beauty of nature', and attributed greater significance to the former. The artistically beautiful, that is the beauty created in art by humanity, was evidence for him of the human being fulfilling his own potential.

The philosopher Johann Gottlieb Fichte, who had died long before the first performance of the Ninth, would perhaps have interpreted a musical world in which all men were brothers as a celebration of the 'I', characterised by world intelligence. For Fichte (and I believe also for Beethoven) the 'I' represents the true unifying greatness of all humanity. The 'I' is for him the continuation of what Heraclitus and Plato called *logos* or reason. The 'I' is greater than the individual; it is an expression of absolute existence. It stands for the person who knows his human potential and is ready to make use of it.

All these fundamental philosophical ideas are for me the basis on which I try to find the appropriate quality of an interpretation of Beethoven's Ninth Symphony. For me, it is philosophy poured into sound. Never has the idealistic idea of humanism been more convincingly, overwhelmingly and comprehensively celebrated.

Up to the present day Beethoven's Ninth has retained a strongly symbolic character. The work lends itself well to the confirmation of social theories and attitudes which place mankind at the central point in its relationship with the world and the universe and seek to lead it towards responsible behaviour. Schiller's text speaks of the ideal destiny of human existence, of ideas of brotherhood and of the consciousness that a higher being governs everything. Countless examples show that these ideas are very often misused, and that illegitimate political systems understand brotherhood in the sense of nationalistic self-interest. Hitler, for example, had the work performed on his birthday by Wilhelm Furtwängler. As a positive counter-example, let us mention those efforts to stress the symphony or parts of it as an identifying symbol of European thought and its notion of peace. Instead of egoistic narrowness, they represent the vastness of human thought and conduct in the sense of world-encompassing humanity.

These are the thoughts that correspond to those of the work. The Romantic 'I', which transcends all of us, described by Fichte, is no mean-spirited ego, not an exclusive but a connecting element. In his Ninth Symphony Beethoven has created a work which for me represents one of the greatest of tributes to humanism. I believe with Richard Wagner, who saw this symphony as the ideal work of art, and for whom the 'release of music from its most individual elements to universal art' had succeeded in this work, that 'it is the human gospel of the art of the future'.

From my workshop II: *Der Rosenkavalier*

For the area of opera, from my workshop I have chosen *Der Rosenkavalier*, a multifaceted *opera buffa* on which Richard Strauss worked intensively with his librettist Hugo von Hofmannsthal. I have many personal memories linked to this piece. I am thinking of the performance at the 2014 Salzburg Festival directed by Harry Kupfer, but the most formative for me was a production I saw as a young conductor. The wonderful Slovakian soprano Lucia Popp filled in on one of the evenings in Zurich for a series of performances, in the role of the Marschallin. When I visited her in her dressing room before the performance to ask her if she wanted to discuss any of the passages, she replied: 'Young man, I will look at you, and you will listen to me.'

I did indeed listen to her that evening, my admiration growing with every bar. She transformed the ageing Marschallin's famous monologue on time into a moment when the clocks actually stood still – a woman regaining her dignity. And then there was the great farewell scene. Lucia Popp sang this with great simplicity, as I had seen her earlier as a great singer of Mozart, among other occasions at the first concert that I was able to attend after my accident. At that time she had sung, with her own deep feeling, the motet *Exsultate, jubilate*, K.165, with the Vienna Philharmonic under Claudio Abbado. Later in my student days in Munich I heard her in the role of the young girl Sophie. Now she herself was playing the Marschallin. And her voice had the same purity and clarity as before.

It is not often that as a conductor one encounters a revelation onstage such as happened that evening. I am sure that everyone in the hall was moved to tears: the audience, the musicians and, naturally, I myself. The reason was that Lucia Popp rejected any form of emotionalism.

No one suspected at that time that Lucia Popp had already been diagnosed with an incurable brain tumour. She knew that this would be her last appearance as the Marschallin. For me personally, this performance in retrospect was the singer's secret farewell to the great opera stage. When it is a question of a human existence, when someone really takes her leave in view of an inevitable truth, she never does this with superimposed playacting, but with unaffected inwardness. It is this quiet inwardness of Lucia Popp that since then I have repeatedly sought in music.

The Marschallin in the *Rosenkavalier* is a woman who has had much to bear with her husband's various affairs, and is fighting for her dignity as a human being. Now she herself is conducting an affair with the young Octavian. He in turn falls in love in the second act of the opera with Sophie, when, in accordance with tradition, he brings her a silver rose on her imminent marriage, as representative of his cousin, the much older Baron Ochs auf Lerchenau.

In the finale of the opera, the subject for me is nothing less than farewell itself, and not only the Marschallin's release of her young lover. I am convinced that here Richard Strauss too was transforming into music his own very personal farewell to the Western world he admired and loved so much, and perhaps even idealised. Even the

Production of *Der Rosenkavalier* at the 2014 Salzburg Festival,
directed by Harry Kupfer and conducted by Franz Welser-Möst

Marschallin's last words, the presumably involuntary sigh of 'Ja, ja,'
which is expressed in the dissonance of a major seventh, is far more
than the realisation that she must give up her young lover Octavian
to the younger Sophie – it is a farewell to the world. At the Salzburg
Festival it was important to me, to the director Harry Kupfer and
the singer Krassimira Stoyanova to spell out exactly this. We were
likewise convinced that the final trio of the *Rosenkavalier* is above all
else an affecting journey out of silence, back into silence: the lapse
into silence of 'Ich weiß auch nix, gar nix' (And I know nothing –
nothing at all), the silence before the dominant seventh chord, then
the trumpet solo that describes the Marschallin's loneliness. Her next

words, 'Hab mir's gelobt, ihn lieb zu haben in der richtigen Weis' ' (I vowed to myself to love him in the right way), which Strauss sets in the key of D flat major, portray her farewell to life. With this D flat major, Strauss creates a connection with the great farewell to the world at the end of Richard Wagner's *Götterdämmerung*, the prototype of the end of the world set to music.

But what is really modern here is that Strauss follows this gigantic farewell in D flat major with an almost hushed ending in the key of G major, which, with the great tritone in D flat-G, the traditional 'diabolus in musica' (or devil's interval), one can only experience as a dissonant interval in a wide arch. The end is described by Hugo von Hofmannsthal in the libretto as follows: 'The little black boy comes in with a candle in his hand, looks for the handkerchief, finds it, picks it up and scampers out.' That Strauss and Hofmannsthal allow such a light-hearted and playful ending to follow the great farewell trio only makes the pain of parting all the greater.

With his operas *Salome* and *Elektra* Strauss had already moved to the edge of tonality. The question of why he then wrote an opera like the *Rosenkavalier*, of all things, is one I consider inappropriate. For me, the *Rosenkavalier* is, despite (or precisely because of) its harmonic reminiscences, a thoroughly logical next step. The sugar-coating that is too hastily ascribed to this opera is only a very thin surface.

This is evident in figures such as Baron Ochs auf Lerchenau. Often he is presented as an uncouth, rustic clod. But it would be wrong to degrade him simply into a coarse Viennese cab driver or an ageing comic figure. Ochs – if one reads the libretto attentively – is a *Hofkämmerer*, a court official, which was an outstanding position, reserved for only seven noblemen. So he knows how one ought to behave. That he does not behave as he should makes things even more unpleasant and underlines the ambiguity of his character. He is boorish, but can also be elegant. In any case he is a many-sided character, who is not only loud. Orchestras and conductors are often unable to resist the temptation to lay it on too thick when he, in pleasant anticipation of a tête-à-tête, sings: 'Keine Nacht mir zu lang' (No night too long for me). Strauss deliberately marked this phrase as *mezzo forte*, while he allows his character to stagger as though tipsy, with the strings playing in waltz time.

If anyone considers the *Rosenkavalier* to be compositional kitsch, they are mistaken. But this prejudice has survived since the first performance at the Semperoper in Dresden on 26 January 1911. There was even a genuine *Rosenkavalier* fashion which suddenly sprang up in Europe. There were *Rosenkavalier* cigarettes, satirical poems were written, special *Rosenkavalier* trains ran from Berlin to Dresden, and one carnival procession is said to have included *Rosenkavaliere* on horseback, followed by puppets depicting Richard Strauss and his stage characters with tearful eyes.

That this opera begins with a bed scene between a mature lady and her young lover was an erotically charged and perfectly judged breach of a taboo. But the *Rosenkavalier* is more profound. Hofmannsthal and Strauss were familiar with the myths of great world literature and, of course, also with the history of music. Their *Rosenkavalier* was also to be understood as a reference to Mozart's *Marriage of Figaro*. Strauss makes this allusion very clear in his rhythms, melodies, and particularly in his harmonies, with all their Mozartesque colourings. But awareness of tradition (such as the relocation of the action to the Vienna of the early years of Empress Maria Theresa's reign) is not a sign of stagnation. Gustav Mahler coined the quip that tradition – especially in Vienna – was *Schlamperei*, sloppiness. In fact, the Latin verb *tradere* means movement – looking back in order to go forward. It is in this sense that I would understand the *Rosenkavalier* as an opera with tradition.

It was revealing to read the correspondence between the conductor of the first performance in Dresden, Ernst von Schuch (he had also conducted the premieres of *Feuersnot*, *Elektra* and *Salome*) and Richard Strauss. Schuch, who worked very closely with Strauss, immediately recognised the *buffo* character of the work. He wrote to the composer:

'I know how I felt when I sat for the first time, at my lonely piano, in front of the score of the *Rosenkavalier* – and thought I was at the Heurigen wine tavern in Grinzing, the whole city of Vienna flying into my house with its eternally young, sweet, carefree life!'

But this local colour is only part of the opera. Together with Hofmannsthal, Strauss wanted to write a work in which every detail grows into a symbol. For this reason, too, he refused to allow even the tiniest of details to be changed. Strauss raged when Schuch suggested an abridged version of the *Rosenkavalier*. And when the conductor asked for one passage to be transposed because of a lack of C clarinets, Strauss immediately replied unequivocally: 'C clarinets are indispensable, please acquire these as a matter of urgency. Transposition impossible. Recommend Oehlers factory (Berlin).' From these small points such as the specific tone colour of an instrument it can be seen that Richard Strauss went to work with uncompromising precision.

At first sight it may appear surprising that in 1912 Hugo von Hofmannsthal's royalties for the libretto to *Rosenkavalier* enabled him to buy a painting of 1912, *Yo Picasso*, by the then not yet so famous Pablo Picasso – and that from then on he became the only Austrian collector of his work at the time. Are there parallels here? Perhaps Hofmannsthal was fascinated by the Cubist painters' practice of seeing pictorial objects from different angles at the same time. A similar aesthetic can be observed in, for example, the *Rosenkavalier*, where we see and share the experience of various scenes from the different points of view of the actors in question. Picasso painted, as he said, for painting's sake, with the exclusion of inessential reality. Strauss also writes music for music's sake. Neither crosses over the limits to which they were already on their way: Picasso never quite crosses the threshold to the non-representational, and Strauss does not abandon the major-minor harmonics in order to position himself, like others, through new rules. Picasso paints Hellenistic female nudes, and Strauss, after the *Rosenkavalier*, increasingly turns to Hellenism. But for both, below these surfaces, the unrest of the time is bubbling up.

What I find the most remarkable is the relationship between word and sound which Strauss and Hofmannsthal have succeeded in creating in this opera. The *Kammersänger* Karl Scheidemantel from Dresden wrote on Schuch's way of working (Schuch rehearsed the opera together with Strauss): 'Schuch's attention was also constantly directed at the clear and beautiful utterance of the sung words. But the whole significance of his musical ability is only evident when it was a question of working out the rhythmic content of an opera. In this respect Schuch occupied a top position among all conductors.'

In our preparation for the *Rosenkavalier* premiere in Salzburg in 2014, quite an essential part of my work was to fine-tune the singers' verbal nuances. With the Marschallin it is a question of an aristocratic-sounding, old-fashioned Viennese accent, with Baron Ochs auf Lerchenau the linguistic range and alternation between the language of the court and countrified speech. But the greatest task is presented by the pair of intriguers Valzacchi and Annina. Both certainly come from a Viennese suburb, but he presents himself as an Italian, and she passes herself off as a different person in each act. It is a great challenge for the singers, in addition to the vocal requirements, to express the equivocal nature of this piece in speech as well. Strauss in addition noted very precisely in the score where the singing is strongly oriented to the flow of the language.

In the *Rosenkavalier* the rhythm of speech and the rhythm of the music are interdependent. When one speaks Hofmannsthal's texts, one approaches the ideal musical tempo of this opera. In this case, one will admittedly not be able to reproduce the metronome indications noted by Strauss – they are throughout rather too fast. But this is easily explained; people think faster than they speak. Since operas are as a rule originated in the head, and the dialogues therefore devised in the course of composition, Strauss was led to create over-rapid metronome indications. Proof of this is found in his audiovisual recordings. In practice, he too chose tempi other than those that he had noted in theory.

Here I would like to make a brief comment on the so-called historically informed performance. When the fundamentalists of historic performance practice profess to know exactly how something sounded 200 or 300 years ago, and this is uncritically received, then I ask myself the question of why we do not at least follow historic performance practice in the case of Richard Strauss. For here is an example where we do not have to speculate as to how the *Rosenkavalier* sounded in its own time. We have access to recordings personally conducted by Strauss – in visual image and sound – and not only of the *Rosenkavalier*.

As far as the words and sounds of the *Rosenkavalier* are concerned, in this masterpiece Richard Strauss and Hugo von Hofmannsthal took the emulation of sound to the limit. While Richard Strauss almost literally adopted Oscar Wilde's theatrical text for his *Salome*, I cannot imagine a text such as Hugo von Hofmannsthal's *Rosenkavalier* being performed as a spoken-word production. It is only the music that ensures the authentic character of the words, and these are mainly noted in a double sense, arising out of the music. For the same reason, also, one should never conduct the *Rosenkavalier* (despite all orchestral temptations) from a symphonic perspective, but always in view of the perpetual *parlando* that takes place here.

'I will look at you, and you will listen to me' – those were Lucia Popp's words before our Zurich *Rosenkavalier*. Indeed it is precisely Richard Strauss's operas that demand a close unity of orchestra and voice. When I was rehearsing *Salome* for the 2018 Salzburg Festival with Asmik Grigorian, in which she became a star overnight, we had the incredibly huge stage of the Felsenreitschule between us. After a fantastic series of rehearsals, in which we worked repeatedly on her role over a period of 17 months, everything now centred on our sense of each other, on our finding ourselves in silent dialogue with each other, even when we could not see each other – it was a question of the unity of voice and orchestra. For this is probably the most important key, precisely for the operas of Richard Strauss.

For me they are a new adventure every time, a highly modern dance on the edge of quite diverse human abysses, and a skilful exercise of playing with noise and the knowledge of silence as the greatest form of beauty.

Going one's own way

The history of musical interpretation is also always a reflection of the contemporary period in question. As in other areas, in music it is often possible to know a movement and a counter-movement, the replacement of one aesthetic by its opposite. After the highly polished interpretations of classical music of the economic miracle period, a new ideologisation of music began in the 1960s. Here too we can identify a pair of conductors who represented this movement in quite different ways. I am thinking of the French avant-garde composer and conductor Pierre Boulez, who founded, among other institutions, IRCAM, the Institute for Research and Coordination in Acoustics/Music, in Paris, and the Austrian cellist, music scholar, conductor and founder of the ensemble Concentus Musicus, Nikolaus Harnoncourt. He lived near me by the Attersee, which gave us the opportunity to get to know each other, but we only communicated on rare occasions. Luckily, to this day his youngest son is a close friend of mine.

Whether it was Boulez with IRCAM or Harnoncourt with the Concentus Musicus, both conductors broke radically with their predecessors' interpretations. With Boulez this is perhaps most impressively to be seen in his reading of Richard Wagner's *Parsifal*, which he conducted at an intentionally high speed at the Bayreuth Festival. Boulez, by his own account, wanted to eliminate all that was emotional or divine. Nikolaus Harnoncourt performed as a cellist with the Vienna Symphony for 17 years, having been engaged by Herbert von Karajan, who was principal conductor at the time. Harnoncourt rebelled, and resigned, allegedly as a result of an interpretation of Mozart by Karl Böhm. In the end he developed a revolutionary definition of conducting. At first Harnoncourt found experimental niches, including Radio Bremen, where he was able to work on his practice of *Klangrede* (music as speech, or music as language). In the first instance he specialised in old instruments and early music, and became a pioneer of so-called historically informed performance practice and a precursor of the musicological conductor.

What these two conductors, Pierre Boulez and Nikolaus Harnoncourt, had in common was that their fight against convention was accompanied by revolutionary radicalism. Other approaches to music which did not correspond to their ideals were denounced by both as incorrect. Many of their self-styled disciples rapidly elevated their methods into dogma.

Much more radical was a similar development with the contemporary music events in Darmstadt and Donaueschingen. Here composers took part initially with the lofty aim of never again allowing music to be used for emotional purposes, as in the days of National Socialism. But this basically democratic idea soon developed into a system of dogmatic rules, which itself in turn developed an exclusion mechanism to which composers such as Hans Werner Henze were mercilessly subjected, because they did not want entirely to abandon melody and harmony.

Despite a certain mellowing with age, Nikolaus Harnoncourt's obsession with research and enjoyment of dialogue have never abated. He was not only a crusading tutor for the famous orchestras of Vienna, Berlin and Amsterdam, but also accepted a great deal from these bodies of musicians with their wealth of tradition. His understanding of music-making became increasingly wide as he gained knowledge. Today it is possible to say that his methods are now established as taken for granted in daily orchestral work. And Pierre Boulez too, who once wanted to blow up all opera houses, later worked in them with enjoyment, knowledge and commitment.

But it is important to examine this chapter of the ideologisation of music more closely. For out of it (likewise as a counter-movement)

Franz Welser-Möst is convinced that a conductor's work in the
long term is incompatible with self-promotion

that diversity has developed with which we are now confronted. For
some, rhythm has become the new deity, others discover melody as a
state of intoxication, some see even Mozart's operas as a quarry from
which they mine what they need as the whim takes them, and others
again try to uphold the dogma of old ideals. By now, just about every
type of approach to music has been represented. Sometimes it seems
to me as though the colourful array of possibilities is in truth only a
refined form of uniformity – wanting to be different, no, *having* to be
different as a collective ambition and a modern profession of faith.

In this situation of arbitrariness it becomes ever more difficult for many people to distinguish genius from lack of knowledge, the charlatan from the serious artist. And here we come back again to the theme of hollow sensationalism, the spectacle and gesture which conceals nothing but a void. Everyone wants the product music, and ends up merely with the packaging. In this situation, ignorance ever more blatantly enters the limelight.

That we are increasingly losing the ability to separate the frivolous from the serious becomes clear from many a piano department at the music colleges, where the piano literature often only begins with Franz Liszt. Furthermore there are trends such as 'postdramatic theatre', which has already left many questions open on the theatrical stage, but is completely impossible in opera: for the drama, the reliance on the text (of the libretto as much as the score) is indispensable. Rapid association and grand effects should not deceive us over the fact that much discipline is needed on the path to interpretation: constant questioning of rhythm, melody, harmony and words, and the persistent attempt to bring these elements into accord with each other. A conductor's work in the long term does not serve for personal fulfilment or image cultivation. The great director Fritz Kortner once said to one of his actors: 'You must not weep, the audience must weep.' And Richard Strauss writes in one of his 'Ten Golden Rules' for conductors that they should conduct the music, not the audience. Both are right: the profession of the reproducing artist requires humility and not putting one's own feelings on show. Rather, it is a question of making audible the complex waves of feeling that we find in the scores and texts.

Our present day is not only the age of multiplicity and diversity, but also the era of high technical quality. 'Actually it is a pity,' a musician said recently in Cleveland, 'that by now every orchestra can play the *Sacre* more or less without problems.' Stravinsky's *Sacre du Printemps* (*The Rite of Spring*), whose first performance in Paris, as has already been mentioned, became one of the greatest scandals in performing history, now belongs to the standard repertoire of modern classical music. The taming of this piece has not for a long time represented a challenge. It is all the more important to realise that today's scandal could perhaps lie in the failure to penetrate a supposedly well-known Schubert symphony and to make audible its unfathomably spiritual depths. For in those depths, I am certain, we find alarming, but also positive statements about human existence.

Perhaps we are now in a state of renewed upheaval. For behind us lies not only the age of dogmatism, but also the age of specialism. The subject areas with which a conductor has had to be concerned have become ever narrower in recent years. We have specialists in Wagner or the Romantics, so-called Mozart experts and Baroque enthusiasts. I believe it is time to understand music holistically again. We have learnt a great deal from the specialists, but now it would be wise to reopen the panopticon, to put the knowledge we have gained in order and to think outside the box. After all, music history has no limits; it simply helps to know *The Magic Flute* in order to understand *Fidelio* – with which in turn one comes closer to Wagner, without whom Gustav Mahler would be unimaginable. And there is no composer who would not acknowledge a debt to Johann Sebastian Bach. To subdivide music history into hermetic, unconnected chunks would be fatal and a total misunderstanding of music history as a continuum. Furthermore one can also learn from the new about the old, from Anton Webern about Haydn, from Stravinsky about Bach, from Strauss about Mozart – music history is composed of an endless number of bridges across time.

The ideal I am seeking also means allowing time for music. It is important to me to take long journeys together with an orchestra, going further each time right up to the next concert. My contract with Cleveland has been extended to 2027. By then I will have worked for 25 years in this city which has become so close to my heart. And I am sure that by that time there will still be so many details that we will rediscover together every day – details that cannot be recognised close up.

In the meantime, the majority of musicians in the Cleveland Orchestra were appointed under my direction, and I am continuously encouraged by the dialogue between older and younger members, whose enthusiasm for playing infects us all. It must always be clear to a conductor that his own position is transitory. But it is a total delight to know that an orchestra has grown in Cleveland through stability and time alone, whose sound we have formed on a path we have taken together – not to mention all those paths we still want to follow in pursuit of our social mission.

The conductor Bruno Walter, in exile in New York, said to another exile from Vienna, the theatre director Ernst Lothar, after a theatre performance which had taken place in German: 'Music is a world language, German unfortunately is not!' The cultivation of this world language is becoming ever more challenging, even in Europe, the cradle of classical music. All music institutions will have to change their structures and internal processes in order to ensure that young people make contact with this art. The public authorities have to a great extent withdrawn from this role, so we need to take over this investment in future generations.

The ideal for me is to have patience, to reject the hectic search for effect, to turn to what has become so rare today – thinking on a long-term basis. For the little questions that pose themselves day by day are the small stones that pave the path to the great whole.

Fourth Journey

Eternity of silence

Silence is a strange thing. Because it has completely different faces. It can, as it were, both calm us and make us restless. Too much silence leads to sensory deprivation, to hallucinations or disturbed thought. Sometimes it is consciously used as a form of torture. But there is silence that demonstrably assists our concentration, and the kind that soothes and lulls us into a sense of security. It is that silence, that stillness, which supplies the German word for the most intimate interaction between a mother and child – *Stillen*, to suckle. Silence can have a punitive effect and embody power, for example when a person being questioned refuses to reply. But it can also express sympathy, for example in a silent farewell. Or it may signify powerlessness in the form of speechlessness.

No wonder that silence in all its forms has always been a significant guiding theme of art: from the Dutch oil paintings known as still lifes, to those treetops over which Johann Wolfgang von Goethe spread 'rest' in his *Wandrers Nachtlied* (Wanderer's Night Song). Silence also characterises John Cage's composition 4'33": the pianist lifts the piano lid (and incidentally opens all the windows) and plays, for the length of three phrases – nothing! The effect is an expression of the dialectic of silence. We do not begin to hear anew until we do not hear what we expected to hear. When the piano is silent, we become aware of the noise of traffic in the street, or the breath of the person sitting next to us, those sounds that day after day fill our silence. For – as some philosophers see it – in the end silence is nothing but a basic state, like a blank canvas waiting to be written on.

For me as a musician it is fascinating that silence plays a significant role, not only in Buddhism, for example in contemplation, but also in other religions, for example in vows of silence. The Second Vatican

Council has even defined silence as a fixed component within the Catholic Mass. Before the confession of sins, after the readings or sermon and after the rite of Communion, silence must reign. It creates a pause in the course of the ritual, and thus an intensive dramatic tension. Precisely this is also an important role of silence in music.

Musicians know that every sound comes out of silence and flows into silence – that a sound, indeed that music is nothing other than a moment in which silence is interrupted. In an ideal case, we think precisely about how this interruption of silence is to be shaped. All this could be compared with life itself: just like sound, we humans too come out of nothing and become nothing – at the beginning and the end is silence.

Hamlet says something similar when, in the last act of the play, during the fencing, he is stabbed with a poisoned sword by his old friend Laertes, and utters Shakespeare's most final sentence: 'The rest is silence.'

Silence too is an experience on the border between being and not-being. The silence of which I am writing marks those seconds in which it was debatable whether my life was about to end or continue – and under what conditions. In the second before our car overturned, I experienced silence as a kind of 'non-time' – as an oversized state which I have since sought in music, one of my greatest driving forces. Here I have indeed often found it in a very similar form. It does not function as a simulation of death, either in music or in any other art. Art, just like nature, can only make audible our emotional state in view of the metaphysical: for example the removal of time or the sense of weightlessness. We discover that silence is a space in which we can have trust, in which depth and fulfilment become possible, for which lack of excitement is true beauty. For this too is part of the multiple dimensions of silence: what is actually loud is in reality silence. Or, as Friedrich Nietzsche wrote in his book *Also sprach Zarathustra*: 'The greatest events – they are not our noisiest but our stillest hours.'

These hours sometimes solidify into moments in which we at least surmise what our targets and ends might mean. Letting go. It is these precious moments of silence which awaken in me a deep sense of security.

Afterword

by Axel Brüggemann

For a long time I knew Franz Welser-Möst only from a distance. He was principal conductor in Zurich when I, still a student in Freiburg, was writing my first reviews, among others for the *Basler Zeitung*, *Die Frankfurter Rundschau* and *Die Welt*. When later I arrived in Vienna, he was music director of the opera there. At that time I was commissioned by a newspaper to write a portrait of him, and I asked him for an interview. If I recall correctly, my first question at our first personal meeting was: 'Why are you so boring, Herr Welser-Möst?'

Franz Welser-Möst had to chuckle, and there followed one of the most interesting conversations I have had as a journalist: it was about the greatness of the small gesture, the importance of the minimal for the architecture of the whole, and the question of the depth of intensive preoccupation. And at certain points it was about everything: the relevance of orchestras, the dialogue between artists and audiences, the question of why we need operas, symphonies, indeed music in general at all – and about how authenticity is to be created in the music business.

After our conversation Franz Welser-Möst and I lost touch, as so often happens in our field. The next time we met, we were standing together on the stage: he was conducting the Staatskapelle Dresden at an open-air concert in front of an audience of 10,000 on the banks of the Elbe, and I was acting as presenter of the programme, which included Dmitri Shostakovich's Seventh Symphony. Before the symphony began, I discussed with music, its motifs and significance, with Franz Welser-Möst, the orchestra played parts of individual passages, and Welser-Möst explained them. It was here that I came to know the facilitator of music, who made it clear to a large audience that had actually come to attend an open-air event how specific every note would be that the orchestra was about to play. Franz Welser-Möst moved an audience (many of whom were attending a concert for the first time) to listen with rapt attention – and this with a long and complex piece of music.

Later I once again visited Franz Welser-Möst in his house by the Attersee for my podcast *Brüggemanns Begegnungen*. And again I encountered another side of him. In his library we chatted about his family's Gugelhupf recipe, about the excitement at New Year's Day concerts, and of course about the appointment of Franz Welser-Möst in Cleveland and his visions of education work.

When, a little later, he asked me if we could not find the themes for this book in a series of conversations, I was of course curious, for I had the feeling that I still did not really know Franz Welser-Möst, this musician whose professional image seemed not to allow any glimpse of his private self.

So we began to meet regularly – at first at my home, for extended working breakfasts, which usually lasted well into lunchtime. I organised rolls with marmalade and honey, and made myself one, two or three cappuccinos – but in all that time Franz Welser-Möst drank, if anything, just two cups of tea. We sorted out the themes and the world of music, but also his biography, and finally decided to concentrate on the autobiographical aspect. Later we continued our conversations, met during his F. X. Mayr treatment course in Innsbruck, went for walks in the snow and through nature, and let our thoughts circle around life, the market and music.

Today it certainly would not occur to me to ask Franz Welser-Möst one question, the one of why he was so boring. I owe so many new thoughts to our meetings, about silence, the small and the quiet, which often receives too little attention in journalism as well. And I thank Franz Welser-Möst for his openness, and for allowing us to examine his past and his life together – the great moments as well as the setbacks from which he was able to learn. And I hope that the result offers readers of this book the diversity with which we approached this project. A book about silence, a book about sound, an inquiry into one's own life, a survey of the soundtrack of our time and perspectives for the future.

Page numbers in *italics* refer to illustrations

English edition published in the UK in 2021 by
Clearview Books
99 Priory Park Road
London NW6 7UX
www.clearviewbooks.com

Original German edition published in Austria in
2020 by Christian Brandstätter Verlag
Wickenburggasse 26
1080 Wien
www.brandstaetterverlag.com

Photography ©
akg-images / picturedesk.com: endpapers
Benedikt Dinkhauser: 51
Gerhard Flekatsch: 99
Barbara Gindl / APA / picturedesk.com: 171
Roger Mastroianni: 32, 103, 108, 157, 163
Herbert Neubauer / APA / picturedesk.com: 131
Privatarchiv Franz Welser-Möst: 18, 23, 35, 39,
48, 70, 73, 111, 181, 188
Michael Pöhn: 93, 113
Julia Wesely: 2, 8, 59, 60, 86, 140, 145, 146, 187

A CIP record for this book is available from
the British Library.

ISBN 978-1908337-603

Translator: Christine Shuttleworth
Designer: Roger Fawcett-Tang
Cover photo: Gianmaria Gava
Editor: Catharine Snow
Production: Rosanna Dickinson

Printed in Europe